Larry King

by
LARRY KING
WITH EMILY YOFFE

SIMON AND SCHUSTER
NEW YORK

Copyright © 1982 by Larry King
All rights reserved
including the right of reproduction
in whole or in part in any form
Published by Simon and Schuster
A Division of Gulf & Western Corporation
Simon & Schuster Building
Rockefeller Center
1230 Avenue of the Americas
New York, New York 10020
SIMON AND SCHUSTER and colophon are trademarks of Simon & Schuster
Designed by Irving Perkins Associates
Manufactured in the United States of America

1   3   5   7   9   10   8   6   4   2

Library of Congress Cataloging in Publication Data

King, Larry, date.
Larry King.

Includes index.
1. King, Larry, 1933–   2. Radio broadcasters—
United States—Biography.   3. Larry King Show (Radio
program) I. Yoffe, Emily. II. Title.
PN1991.77.L3K56   1982   791.44′092′4 [B]   82-10335
ISBN 0-671-41138-1

The author thanks The Miami Herald for permission to quote
from its pages
Copyright © 1971 The Miami Herald
Reprinted by permission

FOR CHAIA, THE LIGHT OF EVEN MY MYOPIC EYES;
FOR HERB COHEN, MY CLOSEST FRIEND, AND AT TIMES THE
FATHER I NEVER HAD;
AND FOR BILL O'DONNELL, THE EPITOME
OF BOTH A FRIEND
AND A PROFESSIONAL BROADCASTER.

PART I

The Fall

ON DECEMBER 20, 1971, I was driving to my evening radio talk show on WIOD in Miami and listening to the station while I drove. Miami is a personality town, and in Miami, I was a personality. In addition to working at WIOD, where I was also the color man for the Miami Dolphins, I had a television interview show on WTVJ and a daily newspaper column—first in *The Miami Herald,* then in *The Miami News,* and finally in *The Miami Beach Sun-Reporter.* During the 1968 Republican convention William Buckley was in town and I had him on the television show. He said jokingly that he was afraid to come back to Miami because he couldn't escape me; I was everywhere he turned.

As I drove to the station that balmy December night the news came on the radio. The lead item began: "Larry King, popular radio and television broadcaster, was arrested today on charges of stealing five thousand dollars from financier Louis Wolfson. . . ."

I pulled up to the station a few minutes after the news. The general manager met me on the stairs to the studio and said it might be best for me not to go on the air that night—or any night in the near future. I agreed to his request that I take a "leave of absence." I also led the news on all three television stations that night. WTVJ decided it didn't want its interviewer to be bigger news than its guests, so it pulled me off my show there. The *Herald* gave the story front-page play the next day, and I got extensive coverage in the newspapers the rest of the week. The *Sun-Reporter* management came to the conclusion that they were giving me plenty of exposure without running anything under my by-line. Goodbye newspaper column.

It was nearly four years after that first story on WIOD before I worked regularly in broadcasting again.

Although I never expected to be accused of larceny, as I look back on it it's amazing that I didn't get in trouble before Louis Wolfson decided to go after me. I have to admit that part of me was relieved when the Wolfson thing blew. For years I had dreaded every phone call, knowing from experience that the person on the other end was more likely to be a creditor than a fan. Hitting bottom was easier in some ways than worrying about hitting bottom.

From the mid-sixties until the arrest (for which I spent ten minutes at the Dade County Jail before being released without having to post bond), I was on top of the world professionally. I had achieved success far beyond anything little Larry Zeiger from Brooklyn had dared imagine when he dreamed as a boy of being on the radio. At my most egotistical moments, of which there were many, I felt as if I owned Miami—and I lived as if I did, too. But as far as my personal life was concerned, it was as if I had a death wish. My biggest problem was money. I felt that whatever Larry King wanted Larry King should have. And

I wanted the best. I got a new Cadillac every year. I always ate at the finest places. I regularly dropped a bundle at the track. When I wrote checks, I never bothered to mark the amount on the stub, which probably didn't matter too much since I rarely had sufficient funds to cover the check. I discovered it was amazing what you could get away with if people recognized your name or face. I also developed a case of amnesia every April 15. By the time my wife Sharon convinced me in 1978 that I had no choice but to declare bankruptcy, I was more than $300,000 in debt. There was no excuse for the way I lived, but I have to say one small thing as a sort of defense: I may have hurt a lot of people, but the person I injured most was myself.

Anyone who has ever gotten himself into the kind of financial jam I was in knows that at some point the thing becomes self-perpetuating. You end up borrowing more and more in order to give the creditors you already have enough to keep them from really taking action against you. And I must say I had a magic way when it came to bamboozling sources of cash. I found bankers, for example, to be particularly easy touches. One routine I pulled a couple of times was to call up the president of a local bank and tell him I was thinking of doing a show on banking and that he'd been highly recommended as someone who could tell me everything about the business. Now, all this was baloney, but the guy would be enormously flattered, so we'd set up lunch. I'd never mention my need for a loan at lunch; I'd just interview him about all the ins and outs of banking. I'd also make sure we ate at a place where I'd be recognized: very few people don't like to be seen with a celebrity. By the end of the lunch the two of us would be great pals, and the banker would have something to tell at his next cocktail party. A couple of weeks after the lunch I'd call the guy back, thank him again for all his invaluable help, then say, "Oh, by the way, I hate to bother you with this, but I wonder if you could give me some personal advice. My mother is quite ill and I need five thousand dollars for an operation—can you tell me the best place to get a loan for that quickly?"

I know this sounds like a bad movie, and it was like one, because just as in a bad movie, the banker would say, "Larry, let me take care of it. What do you need, a thirty- or sixty-day note?" The secret was to get the head man to authorize the loan himself; that way I avoided the standard credit check, which would show I was about as good a financial risk as Mickey Rooney is a marital risk.

Now, one flaw in my system, and it was a major flaw, was that the sixty days had a funny way of rolling on by, and then I would either default, or borrow more money from someone else to pay the note. Another flaw was that there were frequent breakdowns in the system. It's a real test of your professionalism to go on the air while sheriffs are at your home repossessing your property.

In order to keep myself from having any redeeming personal qualities, I was also a lousy husband. I felt that Larry King deserved to be seen with beautiful women, which did not noticeably improve my first marriage. (I consider that marriage my first marriage. However, I was married for about fifteen minutes when I was 18. That marriage, never consummated, was annulled.) Toward the end of my marriage I got involved with the most beautiful woman I've ever seen, a model. Once I took her out to dinner at a fancy restaurant in Fort Lauderdale, where I noticed my doctor and his wife, who were good friends of my wife Alene, a few tables over. The woman I was with had her back to them, but the doctor saw me and came over to warn me that his wife had seen us and to be prepared for her to tell Alene. He walked up to the table, and as he turned to face my friend, I thought he was going to pass out, she was that breathtaking. Years later the doctor's wife told me that she was really furious at me until they walked out and she saw the other woman. She told me she said to her husband, "If I caught you with that girl, I couldn't hold you fully accountable for your actions."

Of course if you're going to have an affair you don't pick a woman like my friend and take her out publicly unless you really want to be noticed. And I did; it was part of the ego trip.

In spite of all my craziness, I was never irresponsible about my work. It was as if I were two people. One was Larry King the total professional, and the other was Larry Zeiger the nobody from Brooklyn who didn't believe Larry King deserved his success. Though I behaved as if I thought I was better than other people and didn't have to live by the same rules others lived by, in actuality I was a mass of insecurities, and I really believed I was the only person to have achieved a measure of success who ever had a moment of self-doubt. It was this feeling of not being up to everyone else's standards that led me to justify my not behaving like everyone else.

While I had been setting myself up for a fall for years, it was one fatal error that toppled the whole thing: I tried to play in the big leagues when I was just a minor-leaguer.

Lou Wolfson, who had made his first million by the time he was 28, was a legendary figure in Florida. He was known as a great philanthropist in the Jewish community: he built hospital wings; there is a Wolfson High School. At one time he controlled a $400-million industrial empire and was known as "the great raider" because of his penchant for taking over corporations. Though he was a multimillionaire, he had a controversial reputation in the financial community; some people felt he had a tendency to upset the apple cart. But whatever he was, he was an important, impressive man. When I met him, he was in his late 50s. He was very handsome, tall and white-haired. He had been a college football player, and he had retained his athletic build. In short, he was a glamorous figure.

I first met him, informally, in 1966. I was, as usual, at the track, at Hialeah. Lou owned racehorses, one of his horses later won the Kentucky Derby, and he had a large private box at Hialeah. That particular afternoon I was passing his box on my way to the betting window when he called out, "You're Larry King, aren't you?" I knew immediately who he was. You didn't live in Florida and not know who Louis Wolfson was. I went over to his box, and he said that he enjoyed my work and suggested we have dinner the following Friday. During the intervening days I think I stopped strangers on the street and told them that Lou Wolfson had invited me to dinner. I knew then that I'd really made it—Lou Wolfson wanted to get to know me! Finally the big night rolled around, and I met him at an expensive steak restaurant on the Beach. He gave the maître d' $50 to show us to the table; he made sure that I saw him give the $50, but it did the trick: I was impressed.

We sat down and Lou looked at me and said, "No small talk. What's your goal in life?" Well, at that point my goal in life was to get through the week without hearing from the IRS.

"I don't really have a goal," I said.

"How much money do you make?" Lou asked.

Miami was a tough town in those days, not a high-paying town. But with the three jobs I was making close to $70,000, which seemed like all the money in the world to me, even though I was living as if I were making $100,000.

"I make seventy thousand a year."

"Seventy! That's chicken feed," he said. "You have to do something in which you have some ownership. You don't want to be working for other people and letting them make all the money all your life, do you?"

I told him I guessed I didn't. Then he said he wanted me to come up with an idea for a show that he would help finance and that I could syndicate. After we batted around a few things, I came up with the idea for something called *Profile*, which would be a half-hour of me interviewing one guest. Lou loved it and arranged for me to fly out to Jacksonville, where his business headquarters was, the following day to set up a corporation.

Now, one may wonder, as I did not, why this virtual stranger suddenly wanted to become my benefactor and career adviser. To this day I don't know. I think it was a combination of things. First, I think Lou genuinely believed in my talent; he was the kind of guy who "adopted" various people and causes. I've seen this desire for control and gratitude in other rich people, and you get a lot of both when you take over someone's life for him—if he's the kind of person who is susceptible to that, and I was. Lou was also fascinated with the media, and no one had more media outlets in Miami than I did.

In any case, I did fly out to Jacksonville and set up the corporation. We even taped a couple of shows which got shown in a few cities; but Lou had other things on his mind at the time, the most important being the government's investigation of him for selling unregistered stock. But I was not the only person, even under those circumstances, whose career Lou was promoting. At the same time, he also financed a series of shows starring author Jim Bishop, called *Jim Bishop: A Critic Looks at the World*, for which I did the narration. Nothing really came of the Bishop shows either, but I wasn't too concerned about the success or failure of these things; I was just going along for the ride.

Although *Profile* never made it, Lou and I developed quite a close friendship. As flattered as I was to be seen with him, Lou is the one who really nurtured it. He would call me up to bounce ideas off me, take Alene and me out to dinner with his wife a couple of times a week. He was fascinated with my shows and would call frequently to ask my opinion on various guests. Once I had Ralph Nader on—this was near the beginning of Nader's national career—and Lou called immediately and wanted to know what I thought of him. I told Lou that I had been very impressed by Nader. Lou said that he'd been impressed too, and a couple of days later he sent me a carbon of a letter he had sent to Nader, which read something like this:

> Dear Mr. Nader,
>   You appeared on my friend Larry King's show recently. Both he and I are very impressed with your work. Enclosed find a check for $25,000 to use any way you wish.

About a week later Lou called me up all excited. Nader had returned the check. Nader explained in a letter to Lou that he had set a policy of not accepting donations of more than $15. He said he appreciated that there were no strings on the check, but someday he might investigate something Lou was involved in, which he wouldn't be able to do if he had taken money from him. He also said that if he took the $25,000 he would be morally obligated to take Lou's phone calls, but for $15 he figured he didn't have to take anyone's calls.

Lou loved it. Nothing like that had ever happened to him before. "Can you believe it, he sent it back. And it was made out to him personally, not his organization. He could have done anything with it," he said. From then on Lou really admired Nader. He was one of the few people he'd met he couldn't do a favor for.

Part of the relationship between Lou and me was almost mentor and pupil. He delighted in exposing me to experiences he knew I'd never had. Once he took me to his horse ranch to watch a foal being born; another time he let me sit in on one of his corporate board meetings. It was all very heady stuff for me, and since Lou didn't like to fly, we would drive all over the state to get to these various places, so we really got to know each other quite well. Lou also liked being a gung-ho fan of mine. Once I wrote a column in the *Herald* in favor of open housing, and Lou had copies made and sent to every member of Congress with an accompanying letter from him.

Because Lou was such a big deal in Florida, and because my friendship with him was so well known, I found myself becoming an important person myself. I was a conduit to Lou and therefore powerful. For example, my lawyer, the late Toby Simon, was also the lawyer for the Dade County teachers' union. At the beginning of one school year the union was on strike over a wage dispute, and had racked up enormous legal fees but had no money to pay them. Lou and I were having dinner one night and he said, "This Toby Simon, he's fighting for the teachers. I'd like to meet him."

I called Toby the next day—all you had to do in Miami was mention Lou's name—and we set up a meeting that afternoon in Toby's office. Lou's first question was how much money did the teachers need. Toby said $10,000.

"Do me a favor, look at that building across the street," Lou said to Toby.

"Why?" Toby asked.

"Just look at it and tell me what you think," Lou demanded.

"It's a nice building," Toby said.

"Okay. Send me a bill for ten thousand dollars. You just did a real estate survey for me. I'll pay the bill and take care of the teachers' debt."

Another time a friend of mine at *The Miami News*, a guy named Hendrik Berns, asked me if I could possibly get him in to see Lou. Hendrik was a Jew who as a young man had fled Hitler's Germany and emigrated to America. He had worked at the *News* for years, but the dream of his life was to have a newspaper of his own. I told Lou Hendrik's story and Lou agreed to see him.

Hendrik and I drove to Lou's house on the beach. Lou ushered us into the living room and looked at Hendrik.

"Did you escape from Germany because of Hitler?" Lou asked.

"Yes," said Hendrik.

Lou then looked at me and said, "Do you like this man?"

"Yes," I said.

"How much do you need?" he asked Hendrik.

"I need fifty thousand dollars," he said.

"I'll write you a check. How do you spell your name?"

No, Lou was not a man for chitchat. I just loved watching him operate; I'd never met anyone like Lou before. I also liked basking in the reflected glory of the "big man."

Following the Securities and Exchange Commission's investigation, Lou was indicted and went to trial on the stock charges. As is usual in these cases, his trial took forever, and because he couldn't avoid flying up to New York from time to time he liked to have me keep him company. One time he arranged for me to stay at the Pierre; Lou kept a huge suite there next to Aristotle Onassis'. The suite offered, to say the least, a different perspective on New York than I had gotten from the third-floor walk-up in Brooklyn that had been my boyhood home. The suite was much too good not to share with someone, so I arranged for my model friend to fly up for the weekend. For maximum impact, I was out of the hotel when she arrived and had the bellman take her up to the suite alone. I discovered that a suite at the Pierre can be a very effective tool of seduction. I should know: I was seduced by it too. After all, the reason I was in New York was that my friend was on trial. However, Lou had told me the charges were groundless, and I was having much too good a time to want to examine things too closely.

My trouble with Lou began innocently enough. I was chronically in need of cash, so Lou started lending it to me to help me keep up with my debts. Because Lou was lavish with his money, and he had far more of it than most people I borrowed from, it seemed innocent—relatively speaking—to me at the time.

In early 1968 I had a guest on my show who particularly intrigued Lou, and Lou asked me to set up a dinner with the guest. He was Jim Garrison, the controversial district attorney of New Orleans. Garrison was conducting his own investigation into JFK's assassination. Eventually he brought a Southern businessman, Clay Shaw, to trial for the murder. The trial was something of a fiasco; Shaw was acquitted, and Garrison was thoroughly discredited. But at the time, Garrison made quite a compelling case for his theory, and there was a lot of public interest in his pursuit. I got Garrison on the show through a mutual friend, Dick Gerstein, Miami's state attorney, which is the equivalent of a district attorney. Dick had been a friend since my early years in Miami. Lou was always a big Democratic backer; he liked to think of himself as a patriot. Garrison was a perfect case for Lou: he was an underdog, he was trying to fight the establishment and he was trying to solve a national tragedy. Garrison was a difficult guy to get hold of, but I told Dick Gerstein that Lou Wolfson wanted to see Garrison, and Dick arranged dinner with Lou, me, Garrison and himself.

It was an incredible night. Garrison's theory, like all the assassination theories, was, of course, incredibly complicated and took hours to tell. And though it's impossible to even barely reconstruct those theories from memory two days after you've heard them, they have a compelling logic at the time. That was the case this night in Miami as we sat in a fancy restaurant on the beach and listened to Garrison weave his story of murder. Dick Gerstein, an associate of Dick's, and I mostly just sat there and listened; the evening was dominated by Lou's incessant questioning of Garrison.

After the dinner we went to Garrison's hotel room, where he played some tapes of interviews he'd done with witnesses. One

I'll never forget was with a Texas pilot who Garrison said had been paid to fly Lee Harvey Oswald out of the country the day after the assassination. The pilot said on the tape that he had been hired by some mysterious men to park a private plane at Love Field in Dallas on November 22, 1963, and wait for a lone passenger, a man who was slight, of medium height and balding. The pilot was being paid $50,000 to take the passenger to Mexico, turn around and fly back. The pilot said that he waited all day the 22nd, but of course no one showed up. At 3 A.M., that eerie tape was all we needed as proof that Garrison had something. We listened to a few more interviews; then Lou turned to Garrison and said, "How much do you need?"

"I sure could use twenty-five thousand dollars," Garrison replied.

(It's funny: so many of the meetings I sat in on with Lou ended with Lou saying, "How much do you need?" and the other guy saying, "I could use . . .")

Lou asked him if he wanted it all at once. Garrison said it was a continuing investigation and that he could use $5,000 a month for five months, and then he'd evaluate his needs after that. Lou said it would be easiest for everyone concerned if he gave Garrison the money in cash. He arranged to give me the first $5,000 the next day, which I was to turn over to Garrison when I took him to the airport. After that, Lou would give Dick Gerstein $5,000 a month and Dick would get it to Garrison. Garrison reported all the money, by the way; he was completely aboveboard about it. Even so, it was clearly stupid for two district attorneys to get involved in a financial deal with a guy on trial for financial irregularities. All I can offer by way of explanation is that there was a lot of stupidity going around, and that the idea that one is going to solve the assassination of the President tends to cloud one's judgment.

The next day I took Garrison to the airport and handed him the envelope with $5,000 Lou had given me. As I was putting the money into his hand, he said, "It isn't going to stop with John Kennedy. Robert Kennedy is going to get killed too." Before the year was out, Robert Kennedy had been murdered.

A month went by and Lou gave me the second $5,000 to give to Gerstein, who was going to give it to Garrison. But Gerstein couldn't find Garrison. This in itself was not unusual. Garrison was something of an eccentric who would disappear for weeks at a time and not let anyone know where he was, so Dick hung on to the money.

Another month went by and Lou gave me another $5,000 to be given to Garrison, but again, Garrison was nowhere to be found. As usual I owed money to the IRS, so I asked Lou if I could pay my taxes with this $5,000 and give the money to Garrison later. By this time Lou's major concern was not Garrison's investigation, but his own legal problems: he had lost in his trial in New York and had been convicted. Lou was an enormously self-possessed man, one who had gotten out of messy situations before, but I think it finally started to sink in that there might not be a way out of this one.

Lou had many influential and powerful friends, but at that time the most influential and powerful was the late Supreme Court Justice Abe Fortas. Fortas was one of the most liberal justices on the Court; a distinguished man who had had a very successful Washington law practice before his appointment. He was also employed by Lou Wolfson. Among Wolfson's enterprises was a charitable institution called the Wolfson Family Foundation. Fortas was paid $20,000 a year to advise the foundation on its philanthropic projects. The revelation of this payment in an article in *Life* magazine in 1969 led to Fortas' resignation from the Court in disgrace.

In a last-ditch effort to save himself—and whatever the courts said, I am sure Lou really did believe in his innocence—Lou called Fortas for help. I was at Lou's home in Miami Beach when he made the call—or more correctly, had

his secretary make it for him. At the very least it was a testament to Lou's influence that he didn't have to wait long for a
Supreme Court justice to return his call.

The conversation was brief. I, of course, couldn't hear
Fortas' side of it, but it was clear from the stony look on Lou's
face that he wasn't getting the response he wanted. After he
hung up, he said in a cold, expressionless voice, "That's
friendship."

Lou, however, was not a man who was easily derailed, and
Fortas wasn't his only friend with political connections. It
turned out that I had one of the best. By the fall of 1968, Richard Nixon had won his long quest to be President of the
United States. One of his vacation homes was in Key Biscayne,
and shortly after his election he went there for a vacation. I was
a social acquaintance of Nixon's best friend Bebe Rebozo, and
I had also had Nixon on my various radio and TV shows over
the years, so when Bebe put together a celebratory breakfast
for Nixon, I was one of about twenty people invited.

One thing Lou did not have was Republican contacts, and
the breakfast was a golden opportunity. After speaking to Lou
about the invitation, I took a briefcase full of papers to the
breakfast. It was a lovely occasion. Nixon was as relaxed and
charming as he's ever been in his life; and why not?—it was
probably the best time of his life.

Nixon made sure that he gave a few private moments to
each of his guests; it was sort of like getting a presidential pen:
it was a souvenir to tell the kids about. When he came over to
me he said, "Larry, I know we don't always agree on the issues,
but I have always been treated fairly on your show. Now that I
have the chance, is there anything I can do for you?"

It was everything I'd hoped for. I said, "Well, Mr. President, there is. A friend of mine, Lou Wolfson"—Nixon indicated that he knew of Lou—"has been convicted for a crime
he says he didn't commit. I have some papers which I think

prove his innocence, and I wonder if you might review them."
I didn't even consider how audacious my request was, and
Nixon never gave a sign that it was out of order. He beckoned
to a bald, pudgy man to join us. When the man came over,
Nixon said, "This is John Mitchell. I think John is going to be
my attorney general. Give him the papers, and John will get
back to you on the case."

Lou was very excited when I told him about the breakfast.
He asked me every couple of days if I had heard from Mitchell.
Finally, about a month after the breakfast, Mitchell called to
say he would have nothing to do with the matter.

At that point I should simply have told Lou what Mitchell
said. Instead, what I did next was one of the biggest mistakes
of my life. I reported to Lou that Mitchell was in fact interested in his legal problems, which thrilled Lou, and as time
went on my story of this interest became more and more elaborate.

Eventually, I said that Mitchell's firm was doing some work
on the case. Lawyers' fees being what they are, Lou gave me
thousands of dollars which I told him I was forwarding to Mitchell's firm as payment. I, of course, used the money to keep
my game of financial musical chairs going.

I've thought many times about why I did what I did. In
some perverse way I think I almost believed my stories; I know
I really did want to help Lou, while proving to him that I was
an important man too. But lying about what I was doing was
going to prove only one thing: my foolishness. By that time,
however, I had gotten myself into such dire circumstances that
I lost all sense of what my actions meant. The only thing that
mattered was keeping the whole mess going another day.

In spite of my supposed efforts, things really began to look
bleak for Lou the evening of his presentence review. Before any
first offender receives his sentence, the court has a process in
which his way of life and family situation are reviewed in order

to help the judge arrive at an appropriate punishment. I was
there the night the clerk came to his house in Miami Beach
and did the standard interview.

The guy had his little form and began to ask Lou the questions:

"What kind of car do you drive?"

"A Cadillac," Lou said.

"How often do you trade it in?"

"Every year."

"What was your income last year?"

"Eight hundred thousand dollars."

"What's your Social Security number?"

"I don't know."

It was an incredible scene. The kid from the court practically passed out; he'd never encountered anything like it.
What particularly got to him was that Lou had no idea what
his Social Security number was: he couldn't imagine a life free
of having to keep track of those bureaucratic details. Lou was
wonderful—very low-key, matter-of-fact. But instead of putting the kid at ease, Lou's manner only made the kid more
nervous by comparison.

Time was running out for Lou, and I knew it. In the final,
incredible scene of this grade-B movie (although I later found
myself starring in a sequel), I went to New York in January
1969 to see Richard Nixon, the President-elect, a week or so
before his inauguration. The idea was to get a presidential pardon for Lou, and where better to go for that than to the
source?

I wasn't even sure I could see Nixon, but I had nothing to
lose. He was staying at my old hangout, the Pierre, which of
course made it impossible to get a room there. I checked into a
nearby hotel and called the Pierre and asked for Nixon's suite.

"Who's calling, please?"

"Larry King."

"Hold, please."

I held and held, getting ever more positive that I wouldn't get through to Nixon—a thought that relieved me no end. After about ten minutes that unmistakable voice came on the line.

"Hello, Larry. What can I do for you?"

"Oh, Mr. President. Mr. President, I know how busy you are, and that you've got a lot of important things to do, but it's urgent that I see you."

"Well, Larry, I *am* flying back to Washington tonight to announce my cabinet, and I'm afraid they have booked me pretty tight. But if it's urgent, why don't you come over to the hotel now. I'm going out for a walk to pick up Pat, and you can come along with me."

It was about seven in the evening, and I ran the few blocks to the Pierre. The place was a mob scene: it was crawling with reporters, cameramen, staff, Secret Service agents and the usual unidentifiable retinue. I announced myself at the desk and took my place in the crowd by the lobby elevators. After a few minutes I was struck by the fact that in the midst of this crazy bustle I was the only person in the crowd without any apparent reason for being there, and I was certainly without the credentials which everyone else sported. In fact, hunched there in my black winter coat with the collar turned up, I looked as disreputable as I was beginning to feel.

Back in Miami I later wrote a piece for the *Herald* (which obviously didn't reveal the trip's real purpose) about how surprised I was that I could just stand in that lobby without attracting the attention of security. The article found its way to the Secret Service, which checked into my story. An agent got back to me to explain that the night at the Pierre the Secret Service detail was from Miami. None of the agents had come over to question me because they all recognized me.

Finally, Nixon entered the lobby and someone came over

and escorted me to him. He shook my hand stiffly and suggested we start walking.

It was a cold, clear night. Outside, Nixon said, "Whatever
this is, it must be important for you to be in this weather when
you can be in Miami." I said that it was. Although the Secret
Service formed a wall around us, the press was following in a
pack, and I'm sure they were all wondering who in the world I
was. We walked for a few more minutes in silence; I couldn't
bring myself to say anything. Finally Nixon said, just a touch
exasperated, "Well, Larry, what is it I can do for you?"

I couldn't do it. I don't know why, but I couldn't bring myself to say anything about Lou. I suddenly realized, here I was
with the future President of the United States of America, and
I was going to ask him to pardon a friend. The absurdity of the
situation—of my whole life—temporarily struck me mute.

"Well, Mr. Nixon, it would really be a big thrill for me if
you could do my show after your inauguration," I said.

"Larry, why didn't you ask me this on the phone?"

"I just had to do it in person."

"Larry, you know I'd love to, but my problem is I can't show
any favoritism with you guys. I have offered Mike Wallace the
job of Press Secretary. He hasn't said yes or no yet, but would
you be interested in being his aide?"

I wasn't sure whether Nixon meant it. I was flattered, but I
wasn't even a fan of his, so I really wasn't interested in working
for him. I mumbled some sort of non-answer. We walked
about another block, both of us wondering how to get out of
this uncomfortable situation.

Finally I said, "I really appreciate your seeing me, and I wish
you all the luck in the world." Then I turned and walked back
to my hotel. As I broke away, a TV newswoman turned and
started to run after me, yelling, "Who are you? Who are you?"
I said to her over my shoulder, "No comment."

Not being able to ask Nixon to do anything for Lou was

probably the luckiest thing that ever happened to me. I don't think my life would have been improved by my being a Watergate co-conspirator.

I flew back to Miami that night. Just as time had run out for Lou, I knew it had run out for me as well. I called Lou as soon as I landed, then went over to his place. I told him how I'd been stringing him along. He didn't make a scene, although I could feel his rage. He simply told me to get out of his house. It was the last time we ever spoke. Shortly afterward Lou went to prison.

I felt a real sense of failure and loss that night. It was one of the lowest points in my life. I wrote to Lou in what I knew was a futile effort to ask his forgiveness. I said, in part:

> I cannot put in words what I feel and I know how you feel about me. . . . I realize that in losing your friendship I lose the best friend I've ever had. This whole mess is surely the saddest occasion of my life. . . . There is no excuse for irrational behavior and if I do not help myself I will always hurt those around me.

Lou ended up at Eglin Air Force Base in northwestern Florida, which is a minimum-security "country club" prison. I knew a guy who served time there for tax evasion. I'll never forget his saying to me after he got out, "Larry, I'm so sorry I spent all that money on lawyers for my appeal. I should have gone straight to jail. It was a wonderful yearlong vacation." He told me that during the time he was there, which was the same time Lou was there, about 1969–70, the prisoners were either businessmen who had gotten into trouble or draft evaders. The businessmen used to conduct great classes there; it was practically like getting an M.B.A. There was one class titled "How to Run a Company with More than 50 Employees." There were classes on stocks and bonds, classes on starting your own business. My friend said that when he was there, six of his fellow inmates were partners in one Detroit law firm. There was a guy there from General Electric serving time for price-fixing who became so friendly with a fellow inmate that he made the guy a G.E. distributor when they both got out. My friend said everyone there was fascinating, and everyone there was insistent he was innocent.

Even in prison Lou was still finding causes. Once he called my lawyer, Toby Simon, and told him to come to Eglin—he had made friends with a fellow prisoner he felt had been given a raw deal. The guy was a jewel thief, and Toby told me Lou said to him, without a trace of humor, "This man never took a thing from poor people."

Before Lou went to prison, he had an associate arrange a schedule of repayment for the thousands of dollars Lou had given me. Although I was sincere in wanting to stick to the schedule, it didn't take long before I fell behind. I was so deeply in debt to so many people that there was no way I could begin to pay off my debt to Lou.

But Lou wanted more from me than money. After he got out of prison, he filed a formal complaint that I had stolen $5,-000 from him—one of the $5,000 payments that was supposed to have gone to Jim Garrison, and which I had kept.

By this time, late 1971, I had gotten the additional job of color man for the Miami Dolphins on WIOD, so professionally I had a lot to lose.

I just kept hoping the whole thing would go away, that I could forget I had ever gotten involved with Lou Wolfson and that he would forget about me. Fat chance. Before the State Attorney's office moved against me, my lawyer, Toby Simon, suggested that I send Lou a cashier's check for the $5,000. I scraped the money together and sent the check to Lou. He returned it with a note saying the repayment was unacceptable to him. I was not about to be let off that easily.

Finally, in late December, Gerstein's office, on the basis of
Lou's complaint, filed formal grand larceny charges against
me. The actual arrest was made as painless as possible. When I
went down to the county jail to answer the charges it took only
a few minutes for me to be fingerprinted, booked and released
on my own recognizance. It was not, however, little enough
time to keep the media from being alerted that I was at the jail.
After I left—sneaked out the back door, to be more exact—I
got into my car to head for WIOD and passed three television
crews on their way to the jail to get film of my arrest. It was at
that point that I turned on the car radio and heard that I was
the lead item on the news—and everything came crashing
down.

It's a shameful feeling to be arrested, but in spite of that, the
full impact of what had happened didn't sink in immediately. I
believed the charges against me were groundless and that once
everyone realized it the whole mess would be cleared up. Even
though I had taken leaves from my places of employment, I
had no idea that I would be virtually unemployable for the
next four years.

I can't take all responsibility, however, for the interest in the
story. When the Garrison story came out, the fact that the
State Attorney, Dick Gerstein, had been involved in trans-
porting Wolfson's money and was now prosecuting charges
arising from transport of that money caused quite a few raised
eyebrows. It turned out that Dick had never gotten one of
Lou's $5,000 installments to Garrison. After hanging on to it
for more than a year, during which time, he said, he repeatedly
and unsuccessfully tried to pass it to Garrison, he returned it to
Lou. In an editorial about the whole matter, *The Miami Herald* wrote:

> • . . . The role of State Attorney Richard Gerstein is a
> peculiar one. As an elected official and the man Dade County

depends on to set its climate of law and public integrity, his involvement is regrettable.

> • . . . Surely, there is some further explanation we have not yet heard. Why, for example, was it necessary for Mr. Wolfson to make his contributions to Mr. Garrison in cash? Why not a check, or a simple bank transfer?
>
> Why would Mr. Gerstein, considering his position, allow himself to become a messenger boy for Mr. Wolfson? Once he got past those questions, we do not fully understand why it was so difficult either to take the money to Mr. Garrison or have him come and get it. By air, New Orleans is a short hop. A weekend, even an evening, would be time enough.

Toby Simon told me that while he thought we could beat the charge by challenging it directly, the simplest and most painless way of dealing with it would be to ask that it be dismissed because it had not been filed within the legal time limit.

While I was waiting for a trial date, Lou wrote to my former employers and told them that if they had me committed for psychiatric treatment he would not press charges against me. Needless to say, nothing came of that particular plan.

So there I was, out of work, charged with criminal conduct and up to my ears in debt. I became, in essence, a hermit. I was just divorced from Alene at that time, so practically the only person I saw was our two-year-old daughter, Chaia. She became a lifeline for me. When I wasn't with Chaia, I simply stayed in my apartment. It was too painful to go out. I was recognized everywhere I went, and people's reactions were either "The poor shmuck" or "He deserved it." I was also feeling a terrible sense of hurt and failure, which was easy to nurse in my little apartment. Strangely, though, as the weeks went by I found myself starting to enjoy my situation. I became the naive little guy who had got burned by the big guys. I began to like being the victim.

Finally the trial was set for a Monday morning in January of 1972. Late that Sunday night, the presiding judge had a heart attack. There I was, back in the paper: "JUDGE COLLAPSES READING KING BRIEF." It was just the sort of publicity I didn't need. The heart attack was not serious, so my case was rescheduled with the same judge three months later. In the interim I went to WIOD and talked to the program director and told him I thought the charges against me would be dismissed. He said the day that happened I would be back on the air. So when I got to the trial I went in believing that in a few weeks no one would even remember I had been in trouble.

On March 10, 1972, the judge dismissed the charge against me because the statute of limitations had run out. What a great moment! All my troubles were over, I thought. I stayed in the courtroom for a few minutes to shake hands and accept congratulations; then I drove over to WIOD, ready to make my triumphant return.

When I got there I was greeted by the program director, the guy who had promised me my job back. I told him the charges had been dismissed and I was ready to go. He looked sick and told me the general manager wanted to talk to me. The two of us walked into the g.m.'s office and he told me that too much had happened, there had been too much notoriety, too many questions raised about me, and they just couldn't take me back. My friend the program director just sat there with his head in his hands; he couldn't help me. Out of the whole ordeal, that was probably my worst moment. I knew then that I was totally alone. I realized that my indictment, as trumped-up as it was, might have consequences I had not been willing to acknowledge. I felt WIOD owed me something, even though I was not under contract. I demanded and got two months' pay. I realized soon enough that two months' pay barely amounted to a symbolic victory. I then figured I might as well find out exactly where I stood in Miami, so I drove to my TV station,

WTVJ. I wasn't surprised when the news director there told me he couldn't take me back either. I had done a lot of taped shows for the station, so as severance I got a year's pay, which also didn't amount to much, as I was only a part-timer there.

That was it. I was unemployable in Miami, the only town in which I had ever been a broadcaster. I was 37 years old, in debt; I had a young daughter to support and no prospects. I felt, in part, that I'd deserved all the rotten things that had happened to me; I'd lived above my means, been egotistical, been a lousy husband. Not that I was ready to be reborn. As usual, I didn't want to think too much about the mess I was in or how I had gotten there. For a long time I just holed up in my apartment licking my wounds. Unfortunately, as far as character reform was concerned, one of the few lucky things to happen to me during that period occurred at the track.

Unlike most gamblers, who will bet on anything—the tables; sports events; when someone will discover George Washington's taping system—I dropped money only at the track. Perhaps it was partially genetic: my father was a horse man, although his interest never reached the levels of compulsion mine did. Whatever it was, I couldn't get enough. I liked the atmosphere of the track. I got to be well known by the jockeys, which gave me a sense of being a big man. I met a lot of important people there, from the great jockey Bill Hartack to the newspaper magnate John Knight to, yes, Lou Wolfson. I liked handicapping: looking at the racing form and deciding which horse is going to win. When you pick the right one, it's an unbelievable high. You can be playing for toothpicks, which I usually wasn't, and when you choose which of twelve animals will come in first, it's a thrill.

So there I was—living like a hermit, broke, out of work—when a friend called and told me to come down to the track for lunch with a bunch of other guys. I said I couldn't—I really didn't feel like going out; but he insisted and told me I had to start living like a human being again. What the hell, I figured, it probably would be good for me to get out, see some friends. I certainly wasn't going to bet—I had practically nothing to bet; it was just going to be a social occasion, sort of therapy.

I got to the track, and before going to the dining room I picked up the racing form. It was just out of curiosity, mind you. I had $42 to my name, my child support was due and I was in no position to place a bet. Lunch was therapeutic; I had some laughs and felt less depressed than I had in weeks. After lunch I decided to go down to the track. Not to bet, of course: just to see a little of the action. I had noticed on the racing form, however, that there was a filly running against a colt in an upcoming race who looked as if she was due for a win. The filly was a long shot—she was pegged at 20 to 1—but I had a hunch about her. Then I figured—just for old times' sake, nothing more—that I would put a $10 bet on her. That left me with $32. I put aside $1 to tip the kid who brought my car around and $1 to get some food. Then I realized: what's the difference between being down to your last $30 and being down to your last $2? The answer was clear: nothing. Since I had brought along the $42 I had to my name, it didn't seem right not to go along with my hunch. I ended up betting the filly up and down. The horse's number was 11. I bought a win ticket on her, an exacta—which means you pick the horses that win and place—and a trifecta. I bought the trifecta on the basis of my birthday, which is November 19: the ticket was for the first, second and third horses to be 11, 1, and 9. I never used to bet superstitiously like that, but I figured if you're going to be irresponsible you might as well go all the way.

I sat down to watch the race holding my win, exacta and trifecta tickets, and my remaining $2. The race started and horse number 1 immediately broke away from the gate and took over the lead, followed by number 9 and number 2. Then my filly, number 11, started to move; she passed the number 2, then

the number 9, and took over first place from number 1. Down
the stretch it was horses 11, 1 and 9, and 11 was so far out
ahead it wasn't even close. That's the way they came in at the
finish: 11, 1 and 9, or 11/19. The win ticket paid $160, the ex-
acta came to $1,000 and the trifecta was $6,432. I had nearly
$8,000. I was wearing one of those tight-fitting jean outfits
which had no pockets, and I didn't know where to put all the
cash. I stuffed most of it into my shirt, buttoned up my jacket
and left immediately. I paid my rent and child support and
stocked my refrigerator. What did I do with the rest of the
money? Within three months I had given the remainder back
to the track.

The funny thing is that I've forgotten the name of my winning filly, and that is something a man who plays the horses
never does. I'm encouraged by this loss of memory; it proves I
have changed: I don't have to hang out at the track anymore to
prove I'm a big man.

As I've mentioned, my marriage to Alene broke up during
the Wolfson affair. The breakup had nothing to do with Wolfson; it wasn't as if she deserted me during my troubles, or she
felt my behavior with Lou had made me an unfit husband. It
was more that neither of us was really committed to marriage,
and we just drifted apart, although we'd been drifting back and
forth for years. There had always been a strong attraction between the two of us. The first time I met her I was moved by
her beauty—she looks like Polly Bergen—and her mystery.
There was a time when we were truly in love; but because of
immaturity, hers and mine, our marriage really never had a
chance. And while Alene's mystery intrigued me, it could also
be a little wearing. She lived very much in her own world.
When we were out for dinner, I would glance at her and tell by
the look on her face that she was lost in her own thoughts and
totally unaware of what was going on around her. She also
acted on her impulses to a greater extent than most people

you'll ever meet. I never knew from day to day whether she'd be home when I came back from work, or she'd be in Rome because something she'd read that day had triggered a desire to be in Italy.

I met Alene during my first years in Miami when I was in my mid-20s. The Miami Playboy Club was just about to open at that time, so I had six Bunnies on my radio show. Alene's cousin was a Bunny—Alene wasn't yet 21, the minimum age for Bunnydom—and Alene accompanied her to the show. As soon as I saw Alene, I knew I had to get to know her better, and after I finished the show I made a date with her immediately. As has usually been my pattern, we got seriously involved very quickly. I discovered that she had had a very tough life: she had had a son when she was 14 and had had to drop out of high school to take care of him. Although she had little formal education, she made a real effort to educate herself. She would go into bookstores and spend $160 at a time. She loved Shakespeare, she would read theoretical books on mathematics—that sort of thing.

We got married in 1962, when I was 28. She had by then turned 21 and was working as a Bunny. I was, I thought, a big star; but I was making $135 a week, and she was taking home $450 a week. When the Playboy Club first opened in Miami it was a real scene—Miami at that time was at its height as a glamour capital—and everyone tipped heavily. I realize now that I viewed Alene as something of an ornament. I liked having this beautiful, sexy woman on my arm. I liked the fact that she was a Playboy Bunny, therefore other men found her desirable. The fact that I had her and they didn't took some of the sting out of the fact that she was making more money than I was.

I always cared deeply for Alene, but I never understood her, never made an effort to understand her. And our personality types were very different. I was an outgoing, pushy, show-business-oriented person. In spite of her working at the Playboy Club, Alene was very private, quiet. Eventually there was too much conflict between my bloated ego and her more private needs, and we separated. Alene started dating another talk-show host on WIOD. I had introduced them, and for some reason it didn't bother me at all that they were going out. I felt that if he was making her happier than I was, it was all right with me. I found out how happy he was making her one night when he didn't arrive to do his show, which followed mine. He and Alene had run away together to Iowa. Now, running away to Iowa does not sound like the height of romanticism, but he was from Iowa and I guess he felt if he was going to do some-thing naughty, he should go home and do it. So Alene, her son and my friend ended up in Iowa, where she got divorced from me and married my friend. When they came back he was very embarrassed and uncomfortable around me, but I assured him that I held no grudge. By this time it was 1967 and I was really flying high. I had my television show, my radio show every night, and I was about to start a daily column in *The Miami Herald.* One day Alene called to ask how I was and we ended up meeting for drinks. I realized then that I had never fully gotten over her, and she felt the spark between us, and so— well, you don't have to be a genius to figure out what hap-pened next: we started having an affair. It was one of the high points of our relationship. Illicitness is a wonderful aphrodis-iac. Eventually we decided to go legitimate and give marriage another try. So Alene divorced my colleague and we got mar-ried again. She got pregnant almost immediately, and within a year of our remarriage we had Chaia. "Chaia" is Hebrew for "life"; it was my great-grandmother's name. We had a very happy couple of years after Chaia was born, but eventually my problems became so overwhelming that I lost my commitment to the marriage, and Alene stopped caring too.

After we broke up the final time, Alene went through a lot

of phases: she lived in Maryland; went to a religious farm in Il-
linois; then to Alabama; and eventually back to Florida, where
she married again. This is not to say Alene is not a good
mother; she is a good mother, very devoted and patient. And
for a long time I knew I would be less capable than Alene of
taking care of our daughter. The only aspect of my current
show that's hard for me is that it is based in Washington,
D.C., and Alene and Chaia are in Florida. I'm very different
today from the person I was ten years ago, and I would love to
have Chaia with me full time. But she spends a large part of
the summer with me, as well as vacations. We also talk at least
three times a week, so there has never been a question of her
growing up without me, as happens all too often when divorced parents live far from their children.

Chaia has not had the kind of childhood I should have provided for my daughter: a stable environment with parents who
have a solid marriage. In spite of that, Alene and I have been
very lucky. Chaia is an incredibly poised, upbeat and mature
14-year-old—more mature at 14 than I was at 34. This is not
to say she has no girlish crushes and giggling fits, which is exactly as it ought to be. She also has a magic touch with animals
and hopes to be a veterinarian. She is the devoted owner of an
Arabian horse by the name of Redneck, and it amuses me, the
Brooklyn boy, no end to have a daughter who is such a country
girl. In spite of my love for her, and my respect for her horse-
manship, she has yet to coax me onto the back of a horse. And
if I have anything to do with it, she never will.

While Alene was traveling around the country during the
early seventies trying to find some direction for her life, I was
making a similar erratic journey. I wasn't ready to say, I've had
my shot at broadcasting, and it was great, and now I'm going
to sell insurance. Since I'd never done anything but radio or
television, I had no idea what I would do if I couldn't get another job on the air. For much of the nearly four years that fol-

lowed my losing my jobs in Miami, I did occasional free-lance writing and broadcasting, most of it sports-related. I've been a passionate sports nut since childhood, so it was an area I knew a lot about and had a lot of contacts in. In 1972 I got a free-lance assignment for a small Miami radio station to do Super Bowl color. I was a little reluctant to take it on. I wondered how the Dolphins and the other broadcasters would treat me—and the station that made the offer was quite a come-down from WIOD; but I was in no position to turn down anything, and I figured the more professional exposure I got, the better.

The Super Bowl was played in Los Angeles that year; it was the Dolphins against the Redskins. I did all sorts of interviews and features for the few days prior to the game and on the day of the game itself. I was under a lot of pressure, because I would have to put together the tapes, drive the sixty miles round trip from Long Beach to the Los Angeles airport and get the tapes on a flight to Miami so they could be aired that night. It was not exactly the glamour assignment of all time.

The first day in the Dolphins' locker room was, as I had anticipated, terribly uncomfortable. For the first few minutes I could read the morbid curiosity on everyone's face. But then a few of the reporters welcomed me back, as did the players, so it turned out to be a lot less painful than I'd thought it would be, although it was clear it was not just like old times.

I had always gotten along fairly well with the Dolphins' great quarterback Bob Griese when I was at WIOD, even though Griese was not particularly enamored of the press. Griese is an intensely private, disciplined person—not the kind of guy who makes good copy, or who seeks press attention. During the '72 Super Bowl many of the players, management and reporters were all staying at the same hotel. The morning of the game I went down to the dining room for breakfast. It was about seven-thirty, a few hours before the game. Griese was sitting by himself having a bowl of Rice Krispies. The room was jammed, but Griese is the kind of guy who can give off "Don't sit with me" vibes, and he was giving off plenty of those vibes that morning. I decided, however, that they weren't directed at me, so I went over, sat down at his table and ordered my own bowl of Rice Krispies. He didn't tell me the table wasn't big enough for the two of us, so I stayed where I was, and we ate in silence for a few moments. Then Griese put down his spoon, leaned over close to me and said, "Larry, can I ask your opinion about something?"

I figured he was going to ask me how he should handle the Redskins, or did I think people placed too much emphasis on the Super Bowl. I also thought I would get some great insights into the Dolphins' quarterback's thinking.

He said, "Larry, do you think property values on Key Biscayne can keep going up? I just bought an office building there, and I've been sitting here wondering whether or not it was a good investment."

Talk about insights. I cursed myself for not having a million bucks to bet on the Dolphins. What total confidence! I knew then that Griese could not lose the game. How could the Dolphins lose when their quarterback's biggest worry the morning of the Super Bowl was about his investment portfolio? And in fact the Dolphins did win, and Griese played an almost flawless game that day.

During the period from 1972 to 1975 I'm afraid I could have adopted as my motto Blanche DuBois's line from A Streetcar Named Desire: "I have always depended on the kindness of strangers." Although it didn't always come from strangers, it was the kindness of others that kept me afloat during that time.

One virtual stranger, however, did—for reasons I have never fully understood—come to my rescue during those years: the reclusive millionaire Ed Gordon. After my experience with Wolfson, one would think I would have been permanently scared off close relationships with millionaires, but Ed offered help, and help was what I needed.

As flamboyance is to Lou, so reticence is to Ed. Ed is very much in the mold of eccentric, very private rich men. There were periods during those years I was out of work in which I must have seen Ed two or three times a week, and I never found out more about his businesses, his marriages or his children than I knew on our third meeting. And yet he would love to have long talks about the meaning of life, politics, religion, history. Ed, like Lou, also had his passions. I was not the only person he took under his wing. While I knew him he had similar arrangements with several women: he would support them and help them with their careers. One woman wanted to be a singer, so he paid for coaching and recording sessions. He was also a hobbyist and collector. His hobbies varied. One year it was model trains. He set up a system in his apartment that was probably worth more than Amtrak. Those little trains were everywhere; he had holes cut into the walls so that they could run through. They even ran through the bathroom. You'd be sitting on the toilet and suddenly, "Choo, choo." His art collection was fantastic, and he really cared about art; it was not just an investment. I'll never forget that the first time I went to his apartment he had a Van Gogh leaning next to the fireplace because he hadn't yet figured out a place to hang it.

I first met Ed, casually, a few weeks before the Wolfson thing broke when a mutual friend introduced us briefly at a restaurant. I certainly didn't think twice about it, so I was surprised when he called after the story came out and invited me to his penthouse for dinner. Ed looks somewhat like the actor Jack Warden, and he is a real physical-fitness buff. In spite of all his money, he liked to do most of his own cooking, which usually consisted of a good-for-you, if inedible, vegetable concoction. However, I was in no position to turn down a free meal. His apartment was spectacular; he had the whole top floor of a building on the beach. Sitting on the terrace late at night surveying the ocean, it was easy to believe you were the only people in the world. Ed's interest in me was sparked, I'm sure, by my troubles with Lou Wolfson. I sensed a deep rivalry between them, whose origin Ed was never explicit about. That first night at dinner he wanted to know all about my involvement with Lou, everything that had ever happened between Lou and me. After I told him most of my story—including my financial troubles—Ed said to me, "How much do you need?"

I know it sounds like déjà vu, and considering what had happened the last time I'd answered that question, you'd think I'd split as fast as possible. I am a different person today than I was then, but not because I wouldn't take money from a stranger. I'm different because today I wouldn't get myself into the sort of jam in which I needed money from a stranger.

"I could really use five thousand dollars," I said.

"Five thousand dollars? What good is five thousand going to do you? I'll write you a check for twenty thousand. When things look better for you, you can pay me back," he said.

I took the money. The next day, my banker, who had been reading about the indictment just like everyone else, called me and expressed some concern that the balance in my account had slipped to $4. Unfortunately, he said, he would have to close it if sufficient funds weren't deposited soon. I told him I'd be in that afternoon.

I went in and handed the $20,000 check, which Ed had written on his personal account at a Chicago bank, to the teller. The teller looked a little startled and said that he'd have to call the Chicago bank and make sure the check was all right. When he got off the phone, about forty-five seconds later, I asked him what the Chicago bank had said. "They laughed," he said. "They said that was petty cash."

Over the course of the next three or four years, Ed advanced me $90,000. When I declared bankruptcy, he was the single largest creditor. Before the bankruptcy I called him and told him what I was going to do, and that it would mean he wouldn't get any of the money back. He told me he had never expected to, and wished me luck on my job with Mutual.

As I had with Lou, I started spending a lot of time with Ed. We double-dated frequently, and he used to have me to nearly all his dinner parties. At one point he asked me to move into an apartment in his building—which he would pay for, natu-rally—because I lived about thirty miles from his place. That I declined. It would have been stepping across a line that would have made me feel like more of an indentured servant than a friend. Ed had a strong need for control and the means to real-ize it. It's a need I understand well. Broadcasting has fulfilled it for me: on my shows I decide where the conversation is going, how long someone will speak, when to pursue something or change the subject. That's why I've gotten such pleasure out of my career; it's offered a respite from what has too often been the chaos of my personal life. Ed and I have spoken only spo-radically since I came to Mutual, but he was a real life saver, and I'll always be grateful to him.

Someone else, in this instance a friend, who showed me in-credible kindness during those difficult years was the great jockey Bill Hartack. Bill and I became friends during the many hours I spent at the track, and he turned out to be much more than a fair-weather friend. It's clear I have an affinity for ec-centrics; I've been close to too many in my life for it to be mere coincidence. Alene is one; Ed Gordon; but Bill Hartack is one of the most charming eccentrics of all time. Whatever ec-centricities may have been lurking in Bill's personality were encouraged by his choice of profession. Jockeys lead a very precarious life. First of all, simply getting up on two thousand pounds of bone and muscle and barreling down a track with eleven other people on horses encourages an inde-pendent, even fatalistic attitude. It's also difficult for jockeys to have a stable (excuse the pun) life: they're always on the road, and they never know from week to week how much money they'll make—their pay is a percentage of their winning rides.

Bill is an unusually thoughtful man who is interested in other things than racing, such as art and literature. He also can be a great cutup when he wants to be, but he's very mercurial, so you never know what aspect of his personality will be at the fore from day to day. I remember once in Miami he invited me to a huge birthday bash his friends were throwing for him. He promised me it would be a super blowout—and it was; it ended up being a weekend's worth of debauchery. The only discordant note in the celebration was that Bill never showed up for it. When I ran into him next, I told him he had missed what must have been one of the great birthday parties of all time. "Larry, did I ever say I would be there?" he asked. "I invited you to my birthday party. I said you would have fun. I did not say I would see you there." Bill explained that on his way home he had gotten corralled into a poker game which ended up lasting the weekened.

Because I was at such loose ends, Bill invited me to join him at the 1974 Kentucky Derby, in which he was riding. I planned to join him for the Derby week, but somehow the week turned into a month. In spite of, maybe because of, their size, jockeys are very appealing to women; there is something exotic and glamorous about a jockey. And the taller the woman, the stronger the appeal, apparently. I have never met so many statuesque females as during my time with Bill. So for me, being with Bill was like being on a monthlong vacation. I'd go down to the track and watch him work out in the morning and, when he wasn't racing, party with him at night. In a way, though, it was depressing for me. So much of my broadcasting career had been caught up in sporting events that it was painful to be at one of the great ones and be nothing more than a spectator.

Since I had nothing to go back to in Miami, Bill invited me to go with him on the circuit for a while, so after Kentucky we ended up in Chicago. In Chicago Bill mentioned to a track official who had worked in Miami that I was with him and looking for a job. The official, Eddie McKensie, remembered me and told me that a new track was opening up in Shreveport, Louisiana, and that I might be good in a public relations slot they were looking to fill. I immediately called the track owners and arranged to fly down for an interview that week.

Shreveport was not like any city I'd ever been in. Northern Louisiana and southern Louisiana are very different: northern Louisiana is Baptist, really like east Texas; southern Louisiana is New Orleans, the French and Cajun influence and a little crazy. Shreveport is northern Louisiana—a direct two-and-a-half-hour drive to Dallas. The interview went well, and I was offered the job about a week later. I was a little hesitant about what I might be getting into. I had lived in urban, very Jewish environments my whole life, and Shreveport was the antithesis of that. Although the job involved doing racing results on the local stations and developing contacts with the media to get publicity for the track, it was also an administrative job, and since I couldn't administrate my own life, I had doubts about that too. But I really had no excuse not to take the job—I'd been out of work nearly three years, and my prospects were not getting brighter; so I decided to give Shreveport and public relations a try.

It turned out to be a good move. First of all, it felt good simply to have responsibilities again. Although I wasn't the greatest administrator in the world, I liked getting to know the local media people and getting press for the track. The track turned out to be very successful; but there were some difficult times when it first opened—which, ironically, made it a better place to work: we all felt we were pulling together to make a go of something. In the fall of 1974, after I'd been at the track four or five months, Shreveport became an even bigger focus of the international sports world. The World Football League, which is now defunct, moved a failed Houston franchise to Shreveport; for the first time Shreveport had its own professional football team. Because I'd gotten well known among the press in town, and they knew I'd done color for the Dolphins, I was offered the job as color man for the Steamers on the city's largest radio station.

You've got to understand that only about two people at the track had ever heard me on the air in Miami. I did local racing results in Shreveport, but that did not exactly make me the Paul Harvey of Louisiana. My relative anonymity was more of a blessing than anything else; while there were times I wanted everyone to know exactly how big a deal I had been, it was also a relief not to have to explain why things had gone bad. When word got around that I would be doing announcing for the Steamers, I got a lot of teasing, particularly about this being my big break.

The night of the first broadcast, I knew in my gut that things would work. When the Steamers rolled out into the stadium, I laid color on them like they've never heard. It had been raining during the evening, and I described the impact of the team lined up against the dark, clearing sky. I gave them the background of the league, the history of the players, the strategy of the team. I was cooking that night.

The next day, back at the track, it was wild. It was as if the princess had kissed a frog and he'd turned into a prince. Everyone there had a new opinion of me. The sports columnist in the *Shreveport Times* wrote that it was too early to tell just how good the Steamers were, but he knew one thing: the announcer was the best. All this newfound respect had a bittersweet edge: a lot of people starting asking me what I was doing in p.r. when I had such a gift for broadcasting.

I didn't give up my job at the track, but I started traveling with the Steamers during their first—and as it turned out, only—season. They played in Birmingham, Los Angeles and Philadelphia, among other places. While the Steamers weren't the Dolphins, it felt good to be back with a team.

This interlude came to an end in early 1975 when new owners took over the track and brought in all new personnel. I was out of a job again. By this time I'd saved about $4,000, so I bundled all my belongings and went to San Francisco, where a friend of mine from the track, Don Farber, was living. I stayed with him while I looked for a job, and after a month or so I landed a spot as the Saturday announcer for University of California football. I had enough faith in myself to believe that once people started hearing me I would be able to get a full-time broadcasting job in the market. Don had a roomy house and offered to let me stay with him as long as necessary. I figured at age 41 I would start a new life in California.

I got the football job in the spring, but because the season didn't start until September, I drove across country to spend some time with my mother in Miami. I took about a week to do it, and it was one of the pleasantest weeks of my life. In spite of all the troubles I'd had and the uncertainty I faced, I felt for the first time in a long time a sense of ease within myself. During that week I had no one to hustle, no one to hide out from, no one to justify myself to, no one to put the make on. I had spent so much of the past few years in an endless hedonistic pursuit—of what I wasn't quite sure. Perhaps all the frantic expenditure of energy was designed to keep me from being alone with myself. On that trip across country I found that I didn't need the echoes of others in order to have a sense of myself.

I faced an unhappy situation when I got back to Miami: my mother's health had deteriorated drastically. We had always been close, and I just didn't know what I was going to do. I dreaded telling her I was moving away for good, but since I couldn't even support myself, I didn't see how I could take her with me. Eventually she recognized that she needed professional care, and she went into a nursing home. One day in the apartment I was helping her to the bathroom when the phone rang. I literally was holding her up when I went to answer it. The person on the other end sounded amazed to hear my voice. It was an old friend from WIOD. My friend was calling my mother to see if she knew where in the world I was. It turned out that WIOD had a new general manager. The g.m. had gotten hold of my tapes and wanted to hire me back. It's moments like that which make it hard to believe there isn't some great plan. I drove to the station that afternoon and was asked to resume my show the following week. I called my friend in San Francisco and the people at the University of California and told them I wouldn't be able to make it back to the Coast.

No matter how low I had gotten, and things were pretty low, I always believed I would make it again in broadcasting. But I certainly hadn't thought it would be back in Miami. I had mixed feelings about my return to IOD. Part of me wanted the vindication, the recognition that the station had made a mistake in letting me go. And part of me felt that perhaps I could never shake the taint of my very public fall. But it was the best offer I'd had, so I took it.

As one can imagine, my return garnered more attention than the average radio-show debut does. The media that had paid such attention to my troubles were more than interested in my return. Both *The Miami Herald* and the *News* did stories about me, as did the local TV stations. IOD fed the flames with a heavy promotion blitz. It was decided that I would do an evening show with the same format as my previous show: first an interview, then calls from listeners. That first night back, it was decided there would be sufficient interest in my broadcast without my having to book a guest. There I was, in the same studio where I had had my greatest success, at the station that had first announced my arrest. I had been away from Miami for several years and, except for the Shreveport Steamers, away from radio for nearly four. As usual, that first night back I had made no plans as to what I would say. I was going to wing it.

I sat down in the swivel chair in the familiar glass-enclosed studio and watched the clock. Finally the hour came, the engineer gave me the signal and I leaned forward into the microphone and spoke my first words:

"As I was saying . . ."

PART II

The Larry King Show

IF I HAD BEEN the kind of person who follows carefully plotted goals in life, I probably would never have taken the offer to become the host of the Mutual Broadcasting System's all-night, national radio talk show. First of all, Mutual's two previous attempts at a network radio talk show—one hosted by the late Long John Nebel—had been dismal failures. And second, I had serious reservations about the concept. What kind of guests could you get at two-thirty in the morning? How many people listen to radio in the middle of the night? And since most radio call-in shows are such local affairs, I wondered if a national one would work.

My reservations proved unfounded. Our guests have ranged from Bob Hope and Bill Cosby, to Gerald Ford and Milton Friedman, to Erica Jong and Joseph Heller. One reason we are able to attract such outstanding guests is in part the answer to my second reservation about the show. In fact, millions of people are up all night: doctors, students, factory workers, insomniacs. Five and a half million of them are listening to *The Larry King Show*. And far from listeners' wanting only to discuss local issues, the intelligence and sharpness of our callers has proved that the American public is happy to have a national forum to air its concerns.

Our show premiered in January of 1978 with 28 stations. Twenty-eight *small* stations. Now, just these few years later, we are heard on more than 250 stations around the country and in all 50 of the top 50 markets.

Ed Little, who is no longer with Mutual, was president of the network when he called me in Florida to discuss starting a new late-night radio show. Ed had owned stations in Miami and Hollywood, Florida, so when he called to discuss the Mutual offer, he knew about not only my abilities, but my problems as well. But Ed had a lot of faith in me—gut faith. He had done no surveys or test marketing of *The Larry King Show*. He just felt I could make the format click.

For my part, I decided I would give the show my best try, and if it didn't work I could always go back to Miami or to another city; I just didn't have that much to lose.

Joining Mutual was not the only major change that occurred in my life in the late seventies. In 1976 I married Sharon Lepore. At the time, I thought it was a sign of newfound maturity that I could be attracted to someone like Sharon; in the past all the women I'd been involved with had had the same sort of devil-may-care attitude about life as I did. Sharon was my polar opposite in many ways: reliable, responsible, good with money, strict with herself and others. She is a former math teacher, and it shows. She is also a stunning blonde who could be taken for the sister of her two teen-age daughters.

When I met Sharon we were both at turning points in our lives. I had just come back on the air a few months before; she was in the middle of a divorce from her husband, who had been her *junior* high school sweetheart.

Sharon grew up in Chicago, but her husband, an insurance executive, had been transferred to Florida shortly before we met. Soon after they moved there, the marriage broke up. A friend of mine, a lawyer named Neil Sonnett, had been casually dating Sharon since her separation. I had known Neil for years, actually since he was the captain of his high school debating team, and he had appeared on one of my earliest radio shows in Miami. So Neil and I really went way back. One evening in late 1975, Neil took Sharon and a girlfriend of hers out for a night on the town. They ended up at an all-night restaurant near WIOD, and Neil suggested at about 4 A.M. that they all go over and watch a radio show in progress. Four A.M. tends to be crazy time on the radio, so when they showed up I immediately put Neil—a fine, upstanding lawyer—on the air and told him to give the history of the birth of the Constitution. Considering the hour, he didn't do too badly.

As soon as I looked at Sharon, I was immediately attracted to her. That's always the way it's been with me. If it doesn't click immediately, it's never going to. When the break for the news came, I introduced myself to Sharon and her friend and then hustled Neil to the men's room. I asked him how serious he was about Sharon. He said he wasn't. I asked him if he minded if I asked her out, and he said if it was all right with her it was all right with him.

I called her two days later, but for a variety of reasons we kept missing each other's calls or were unable to find a time both of us were free, so I finally gave up. About three months later, in January of 1976, something prompted me to call Sharon again. She was surprised to hear from me, but this time we made plans. On our first date I took her to a place called Joe's Stone Crabs. It's not an elegant or romantic restaurant, but it's a very popular place that has great food and a fun,

charged-up atmosphere—which can sometimes be more con-
ducive to romance than a highly romantic place. I had known
the owners of the place for a long time and called and told
them I was bringing someone special for dinner and I wanted
them to lay on the whole treatment. And VIP treatment we
got. Even though there was a long line in front of the restaurant, we were whisked right in and given a great table. Everything went right that night, including the chemistry between
Sharon and me.

From that night on it was a whirlwind courtship. I wined
and dined her, made sure she met interesting and influential
people and generally presented myself as being a hell of a lot
more important than I was. I think we each represented to the
other the chance to have a different kind of life than we'd led
before. Sharon's first husband was staid, conservative, a real
junior-executive type. Sharon was, as I've said, much more serious and responsible than anyone I'd ever been involved with
before.

Sharon was having some trouble with her divorce, so I got a
lawyer I knew to handle her case for her. He also happened to
have been the judge who had dismissed Wolfson's charges
against me, now returned to private practice. Miami could be a
small town in some ways. Shortly after Sharon's divorce became final, we got married in September of 1976.

In so many fairy tales the story ends with the wedding day,
leaving the couple presumably to live happily ever after; after
all, the courtship is the important part, right? As anyone who's
ever been married knows, courtship is a breeze compared with
the reality of sharing your life with someone day in and day
out. For Sharon and me, marriage meant some difficult adjust-
ments. The differences in personality that we each found appealing in the other when we were dating became a source of
tremendous conflict as we attempted to mesh our different ap-
proaches to life. We fought over the discipline we should

or should not impose on the children. (Sharon's daughters, Lori and Linette, were 13 and 10 when we got married, and Chaia was 8.) We fought about money. We fought about our basic approach to things. There was also the problem that Sharon put her finger on one day by saying that I'm a better date than a husband. I am a great date. I'm attentive, extravagant, entertaining. It's hard to maintain the same level of effort when one is married, however, which leads to a feeling of being let down on the part of the recipient of all this attention.

I do have to take the blame for the early difficulties. Right away we were faced with a crisis. When I was taking Sharon out it was important to me to come across as a "big man." And "big man" meant to me that I made a lot of money and spread it around lavishly. I had told Sharon I was making $50,000 a year, and if I had been, I would have been lucky if that had covered all my expenses; actually I was making closer to $28,-000. Because I'd been out of work and out of Miami for so long, it had been fairly easy to avoid my creditors. But as soon as I came back to Miami, they sprang to life again. I tried to keep the situation from Sharon as much as possible, but it didn't take too long for her to find out how much I was really making and how much I owed. This was a real testing point in our very new marriage. She felt betrayed by me, and she was also appalled, never having been close to someone who didn't handle his finances properly. It was also terribly painful for me to have to admit to someone I cared about that I was not exactly what I had said I was. But the good thing to come out of this was that I saw I couldn't, as I had always done, lie my way out of this situation. Sharon was someone who was not going to believe any more lies, who would not stand for them.

By the time I went to Mutual, Sharon had made it clear that I had to resolve my financial mess, and the only way to do it and be able to make a new start was to declare bankruptcy. There have been a couple of stories in the press since the success of the Mutual show that I declared bankruptcy when I did so that I could kiss off all my creditors and be free to rake in big bucks from Mutual. That simply is not true. At the time I declared bankruptcy, I was making $50,000 a year at Mutual. The show was just starting, and I had absolutely no guarantee that it would last beyond the first twenty-six weeks. Realistically, there was no way I could pay back the $300,000 of debt (including $90,000 to Ed Gordon, who forgave any obligation) I'd accumulated over the years. And since declaring bankruptcy I have been reasonably able to stay out of debt.

Although the move to Washington for the Mutual show meant new exposure and success for me, in the beginning it was very difficult for Sharon; she didn't know anyone here and was at loose ends as far as her role in life was concerned. Her daughters were old enough so that they didn't need a full-time mother, and Sharon was not interested in resuming her teaching career. And in spite of my new success, the hours of the job put a special strain on the marriage. We could never spend an uninterrupted evening together or go to a party without my having to leave early. And, of course, I spent the morning catching up on sleep.

Gradually, though, Sharon started making a place for herself. The most important step was her getting a job on the production end of *The Charlie Rose Show*, a syndicated talk show out of Washington. Sharon also discovered an interest in being in front of a microphone herself, and with my help did a local cable talk show and some substituting on local radio shows.

Sharon's new career led to what was for me the most stable phase of our marriage. For the first time she truly saw the pressures and demands of the business and understood why I couldn't live the life of an insurance executive. But I found out that the placidity in our relationship was only on the surface. Sharon's newfound independence gave her the means to end a marriage she apparently hadn't been committed to for quite a while. In early 1982 when the possibility that Chaia might live with us arose, Sharon reacted very negatively. She said she didn't want to take on the responsibility of another teen-ager and suggested I take an apartment for a short period while we worked out the decision about Chaia. Almost immediately after I moved out, Sharon filed for divorce.

It is never pleasant to end a marriage. I know: I've ended my share of them. Ironically, the bitterness of our parting has made ending this marriage easier. The anger tends to drown out any regret that might surface.

Should Sharon and I have ever been married? Probably not. But I don't regret having made the marriage. She was good for me in a lot of ways—she forced a discipline on me, financially at least, that I much needed. But right now I am happy to be single. It is delightful not to have to account for my every waking moment and not to feel responsible for someone else's. I have always been good at living alone, and I foresee doing a lot of it. However, I have intense feelings about Sharon, and you never know.

ALTHOUGH THE SPECIAL QUALITY of any talk show rests with the man or woman who asks the questions, a major component in the success of *The Larry King Show* is its format. The show airs from midnight to 5:30 A.M. EST, and is divided into three distinct sections. First, there is an hour in which I interview the guest; second, from 1 to 3 A.M. the guest takes calls from people all over the country; and third, from 3 A.M. until sign-off is "Open Phone America." During "Open Phone" the guest has departed, and I take calls on any and every—and I mean every—topic. It is a nightly happening that can have me dealing with such subjects as baseball, the Social Security system, the Middle East and growing up in Brooklyn.

People who have appeared on the show almost universally remark upon the intelligence and sophistication of the callers, as opposed to the kooks who populate many local radio talk shows. Our show does get the occasional kook, but for the most part listening to the callers can restore your faith in the quality of the American people.

Our show has also become, in some ways, a national town meeting. We offer an opportunity for people from all over the country to voice their reactions to the events of the day, as well as issues that might not be on the front page. Because of this, major news organizations often monitor our show to get a spontaneous look at what Americans are thinking. Ted Koppel says he listens to the show on his way home from *Nightline*. And one *Newsweek* reporter who happened to be tuned into "Open Phone America" one night got a scoop because of it.

One Friday night early in the summer of 1979, a man from Los Angeles called about 4:30 A.M. EST. He said, "Larry, you having any trouble getting gas?"

"I don't know what you're talking about, sir," I replied.

"Well, it was the strangest thing. When I drove home tonight, there must have been twenty cars lined up at every gas station I passed. I had to wait an hour to get my tank filled."

"Did you ask the attendant what the trouble was?"

"No. I was so mad by the time I got to the front of the line that all I wanted to do was get out of there. But I just wondered if anyone else had the same problem, because I'm telling you, there's something strange going on in Los Angeles."

A few minutes later a guy from Phoenix called and said the Los Angeles guy must be crazy; no one he knew was having any trouble getting gas.

I didn't think any more of it, but a *Newsweek* reporter in Washington did. He called the L.A. bureau the next day, and the L.A. bureau said that yes, something had burst on Friday and it was suddenly practically impossible to get gas. So *News-*

week was able to get a little box in that Monday's issue about the gas shortage. It was the first national coverage of what turned out to be one of the biggest domestic stories of that summer.

Because the show gives such immediate feedback on the day's events, it can be a real barometer of the public's mood. The night the hostages were taken at the American Embassy in Teheran was one of the most incredible nights I've ever spent on the air. It was a big story, there was no question about it. But my show provided the first indication that the hostage crisis, as it came to be known, was to become the focus of so much American rage.

All the calls—all the calls that night, and the next three nights—were about the hostages. I've never heard so much anger. I was really floored; if you think about it, the taking of the hostages was an outrageous act, and terrible for the embassy personnel involved, but it was not the worst thing to have happened to the United States. I think any Carter Administration officials who might have been listening realized then that this would be an issue people wouldn't forget about. And the calls went on for days. I tried to make something constructive out of it, to ask people what it was they wanted; should we bomb Iran, for instance. Most people did not advocate military action, at least not in the early days. What made people so angry was that they didn't know *what* to do; they just couldn't believe a bunch of terrorists could humiliate the United States that way and get away with it.

"Open Phone America" can also tell you a lot about the country by what people *aren't* saying. I should have known early on that Ronald Reagan was going to win the landslide victory that he did. In all the months that people called about the 1980 election, the way they felt about the issues and the candidates, I can hardly remember anyone's saying, "I think Jimmy Carter has done a great job, and he's got my vote."

People were calling and saying great things about Reagan, or that they had reservations about Reagan but were inclined toward him, or even that they had no idea what to do when they went into that booth. But I never heard from any core of people who supported the incumbent President. And if an incumbent President doesn't have supporters who would make their views known on a program such as ours, you know the man has got to be in trouble.

Another night that reached the same pitch as the night the hostages were taken was the night John Lennon was killed. Again, every call was on that subject, and the outpouring of emotion was incredible, sometimes painful, to listen to. Lennon was a musician I respected, but because of my age, not one who articulated an attitude or marked the moods of my youth the way Sinatra had done for me; but I had a lot of compassion for the people who called that night. At one point Milton Berle called from California and he said there was a feeling in the show-business community that no matter what one's generation or type of music, one of their own was taken from them that day.

Many people were crying, or really at a loss for words, that night, but I let the calls go a little longer than I usually do because the feelings were so deep. I felt that I was offering a catharsis for these people; that in some way they were able to share their pain, and try to get some grasp of what had happened, through my show.

PEOPLE OFTEN ASK what subject comes up most often during "Open Phone." Money is far and away the subject most on people's minds. People are terribly anxious that no one really knows why the economy is out of control, and what must be done to get inflation licked and productivity up. But often

people are concerned with money because it is the most immediate reflection of what they see as a loss of the American vision: a sense that we can do anything, and do it best, as long as
we set our minds to it, and a concurrent belief in our goodness
and rightness. People have less confidence about their future;
they know things won't necessarily get better; they see year
after year that their money is worth less and less. Twenty years
ago when someone bought a house with a thirty-year mortgage,
he thought about that thirtieth year: "I'm 24, and when I'm
54, the house will be mine." I think the uncertainty about
what used to be our most stable institutions has led to the
growth in fundamentalism and the Moral Majority: the people
who want to ban books, who are terrified of evolution's being
taught, who want to dictate what you can see on television. I
get quite a few of those people calling in, and the thing I've
found is not that they are full of hope and optimism because
they have found the "right way," but that they are terribly
afraid and pessimistic. They don't believe in the system, in the
Constitution; they have to ram their beliefs down everybody
else's throat. They are grabbing on to God because they don't
want to face the world—or they use this belief in God to justify anything they do. I don't doubt their sincerity—they are
sincere—but I think they are also preyed upon; fortunes are
being built on their readiness to contribute to ultraconservative
organizations.

In spite of my being one of the last unrepentant liberals,
fundamentalists do listen to the show apparently, because I get
quite a few letters from people who have listened to me express
my opinions and write to say they are praying for me, and they
usually enclose a Bible. I get several Bibles a week this way. To
be fair, I have to say that "evangelical" atheists are just as bad
as fundamentalists in their need to make the world conform to
their point of view.

I think people's fascination with sports reflects the same sort of dissatisfaction with the world that makes people turn to fundamentalism. I know when I was a boy my interest in sports, particularly baseball, was a great escape from whatever problems I had to confront, and I think their ability to lift people out of their concerns keeps sports from being a pastime of just the young. On any given night on "Open Phone" I probably get nearly as many calls on sports as I do on the economy or other political subjects. I remember one night I got four calls in a row about baseball. The fifth caller said, "I was going to call in about another topic, but now my question is why someone would take the time to call you, Larry, to talk about baseball. Look around in this world—we probably won't all be here in twenty years; if we don't poison ourselves to death with pollution, it's likely that we'll end up bombing ourselves off the face of the earth—but all anyone wants to talk about is baseball."

"That's why they're calling about baseball—because of all the things you just said," I replied. And I really believe it. Baseball is one of the few constants in life; the men in that park are playing a game the same way it was played fifty years ago. It's a civilized game; there's no violence to it, and although there is drama to a baseball game, it is a relaxing sort of drama. You can go get a hot dog in the middle of the game and be pretty certain that nothing crucial will have happened while you're gone. There are no clocks at ball parks; they are going to play the game until one side wins. That could be nine innings, it could be twelve, and while you're there, you're not under the pressure of the clock, and you're not going to think about a nuclear plant leaking, or the Russians, or inflation.

"Religion is not the opiate of the masses," I said to the caller, "sports are. Sports are a worldwide opiate. I'm reading *Gorky Park* now, and in the detective's wanderings through Russia he goes into bars, and if a hockey game is on, people are screaming and betting and going crazy over it. In South

America soccer is as important as the Church. People don't want to face the real difficulties of life: that's why sports are so unimportantly important."

If money and sports are two of the biggest topics on the minds of the callers, the one you would expect would be the natural partner, sex, is not. By sex, I don't mean people calling for advice on impotence or that sort of thing: I mean a discussion of sex roles, of where women are in society, if men really are becoming more concerned with family and home. But for whatever reason, and I don't know what it is, I get very few calls on that subject. If I have a guest who is dealing with interpersonal issues, then there will be calls, but there are very few spontaneous calls on that subject. Think back on the anger, the passions that were raised by the women's movement. That has cooled. I guess in one way that means that a lot of the changes women fought for so bitterly in the sixties and seventies have been accepted.

Of course, not all the calls to the show are of a serious nature. We have what I think of as a very loose, widely scattered comedy troupe which periodically calls the show. These people never get together, but they all have similar wacky senses of humor and I think of them as a group. I don't like repeat callers on my show—it becomes too monotonous when you have a national audience—but I make an exception with this handful. They are the Portland Laugher, the Syracuse Chair, the Miami Derelict and the Brooklyn Scandal Scooper.

It's difficult to be a regular on my show, so the fact that these people get in fairly often is a testament to their persistence. On a local talk show a caller can probably get in a couple of times a week. On my show a regular is someone who calls once a month. Mostly this is due to the volume of calls we get. I have a fifteen-button telephone in front of me when I do the show, and from the moment we go on the air every line is flashing, and we don't even start answering calls until an hour into the show. About a hundred callers get through in a night; thousands try. Our area code is the busiest in the country at night because of the show. The phone company has had to install special equipment to handle the load. In the beginning there was more than one occasion when 703 blew—no one could make a call in an area that includes the Pentagon and the CIA.

The Portland Laugher is a guy who has called nearly since the debut of the show, and I have never heard his speaking voice. He is as described: he simply laughs. But he has one of the world's great infectious laughs, so we've worked out a little routine. We don't screen the calls to the show—that is, ask the people what they want to talk about before they get on. We simply ask them where they're from. Colleen Moran, the studio director, takes the calls and tells me through a headphone the town of the caller so I can say, "Memphis, hello," or "Providence, hello." Whenever Mitch says Portland's next, I prepare myself for the Laugher. When I hear it's the Laugher, I do two things: first I ask him a serious question; then I ask him a lighter question. For example, I'll say, "Sir, what do you think of President Reagan's economic plan?" and the Laugher practically passes out from laughing. Then I'll say, "What do you think of the abilities of baseball commissioner Bowie Kuhn?" and the Laugher will get hysterical again. I always hang up on him during the second laugh.

The whole routine sounds silly, but for some reason it really works, and if I haven't heard from the Portland Laugher in a while, other listeners will call and ask where he's been. One guy from Florida called up and said he'd named one of his racing greyhounds "The Portland Laugher" and he called us back the night the dog won its first race.

The Syracuse Chair started during the ill-fated prospective debate between candidates Ronald Reagan, John Anderson, and Jimmy Carter. Carter said he wouldn't agree to the debate if third-party candidate John Anderson was included, and for a while the League of Women Voters, which was sponsoring the debate, threatened to put an empty chair on the stage where Carter was supposed to be. Ultimately Carter didn't debate, but the League didn't embarrass him with an empty chair.

The first time the Chair called was just after it was announced that there would be no empty chair on stage. When I said, "Syracuse, hello," he said, "Larry, this is the Chair. I'm really down in the dumps, Larry. I got all shellacked, varnished, this was going to be my big break, and at the last minute they cancel me. I'll never get a break like this, Larry." The guy was awfully clever, so I decided to go with it. I said, "Well, things do look bad for '80, but do you have any plans for the next election?"

"Well," he said, "I am thinking of giving it a try in '84, so I have to start looking for an ottoman to run with me."

I thought the election would mean the end of the Chair, but he's managed to keep the thing going. One time he called and said he was working on his platform. "How's this?" the Chair asked. "The chair's the most reliable thing in American life. Your feet hurt? You sit down in a chair and you feel better. There's always a chair around when you want one; chairs never bother you. When was the last time you heard of a chair starting a war?"

Now he calls with news of his efforts to get better known in political life.

"Larry, this is the Chair. Guess who sat on me today?" he opened one call. "Senator Bill Bradley of New Jersey. I was in Washington, just catching up on the scene. I was in the outer area of his office and some of his constituents were there and he just came and sat on me. It was a big thrill, Larry. Though it was something of a strain; the guy's a former basketball player. You know, I've touched some of the major political figures of our time, and from a weird position."

The Miami Derelict is a guy who claims, and I believe him, that he stays home every day and tapes radio and television shows. He has the most incredible library of recordings I've ever heard. What the Derelict does is call and run a tape that's appropriate to the subjects that have come up during "Open Phone." One night after a discussion of baseball he called and played the tape of New York Giant Bobby Thompson's home run that took the 1951 pennant from the Brooklyn Dodgers. Talk about memories! That tape brought back one of the worst moments of my life. When the Dodgers lost, people took numbers to get in line to jump off the Brooklyn Bridge.

He calls himself the Derelict because he doesn't work, he just tapes. To show you both the comprehensiveness of the Derelict's collection and the devotion of some listeners, the Derelict called one night with a recording of the announcement of the canine version of the Portland Laugher winning its first race. (Dog and Derelict are both Floridians.) The Derelict, like the other regulars, calls almost exclusively during "Open Phone," but one night during the call-in segment of the interview the Derelict phoned. The guest was Kathy Cronkite, Walter's daughter, who had just written a book about growing up with a famous parent. When I heard the caller say, "Hello, Larry, it's the Derelict," I almost cut him off, because I couldn't imagine what he would have to say to her. But before I did, the Derelict said, "No, Larry, hold on, I've got something for your guest," and he played the last minute of Cronkite's final evening news broadcast. She was delighted.

The Brooklyn Scandal Scooper is an unemployed dishwasher who wants to get into radio. He's a bright guy: why he's washing dishes I don't know. Now, the Scandal Scooper's fame is not limited to appearances on *The Larry King Show*. To fans of the New York Rangers hockey team he's known as the Ranger Fanatic. He runs around the stands in an Indian headdress, and he's such a spectacle that he invariably gets on camera when the Ranger games are being broadcast. I found all this out one night at a Rangers game when he came over and introduced himself. But when he calls my show he identifies himself as the Scandal Scooper. What the Scooper does is tell jokes—usually lousy ones—and ask the "studio audience" to rate them. The Scooper seems undaunted by the fact that the "audience" almost always pans him.

The thing with the "studio audience" is part of the fun that I have with the show, and that you can have with radio. The two great advantages of radio that my show demonstrates are time and imagination. If you're a guest on the *Today* show or *Good Morning America* and you get five minutes, you're on for a very long time. Fifteen minutes is generous on most television talk shows. On my show a guest gets three hours; you can learn an awful lot about someone in the course of three hours. And I think the fact that my show is on late at night is another plus; defenses start to break down after midnight. The hour also works to our advantage in another way. When people are listening at two or three in the morning there usually aren't a lot of distractions around; our show gets much more concentrated attention than most television shows. Radio is also the most personal, intimate medium there is, for both the participants and the listener. It's terribly unnatural to be made up and worry about camera angles—Will they do a close-up if I scratch my nose? That sense of the artificiality of television translates itself to the listener. On radio, it's just me and the guest sitting and talking; my guests don't have to worry about how they look, their facial expressions. And the listeners aren't distracted by that either—they won't get turned off to a guest because they don't like his tie, or the way she does her hair. Because listeners to radio do not see the people, it becomes more of a theater of the mind to them. In a strange way, that gives them a greater sense of involvement than they can get from watching television. I remember the late Rod Serling saying once on my show in Miami that radio was inherently more dramatic than television. If he wanted to set a show in an isolated castle, with a few words and some sound effects he could give enough of the mood of the castle so that people imagined their own castles, which would be much scarier than any set he could create for television. And once you show that television castle, it's fixed; viewers aren't exercising their own creativity, and a sense of participation is lost.

I try to use the imagination and sense of participation that radio sparks. For example, there is no studio audience at *The Larry King Show*—all we have is canned tapes of different sorts of crowds: cheering, booing, yawning. It's a classic radio device, but it still works; it's so canned-sounding that people can enjoy the tease, as well as cheer or boo or yawn along with it.

The audience is not the only tape we use as a running gag. Probably the most popular one is the tape of the president of Mutual, Martin Rubenstein. In it Mr. Rubenstein is unable to speak, because he is subject to laughing fits that would put the Portland Laugher to shame. No matter what I ask him, we can never get anything more than helpless laughter out of him. The listeners love the Rubenstein tape, and often have questions to put to the president of the network so they can hear his crazy laugh. People love that gag so much because everyone wants to have fun at the boss's expense. I have to say that when I started this gag, I did not know Marty well, and was somewhat concerned about his reaction; but he's been wonderful about it, although I don't think he is totally appreciative of the notoriety it's brought him. We also have a Mutual Symphony Orchestra tape, which sounds like two kazoo players with bronchitis. One of the nice things about gags like these is that they allow some creativity on the part of the engineer; he or she often decides what tape to run and when, and if an engineer comes across something he thinks might work as a bit, he's encouraged to use it.

Because the show is so loose, we can do quirky things, or go with mistakes. One night the engineer hit the trigger on Rubenstein's laugh and nothing happened; there was a malfunction somewhere. So I went with it. "Mr. Rubenstein, Mr. Rubenstein, are you there?" I said. "Oh, my God, the president is missing! Mutual is without its leader." Then people started calling with guesses as to where he might have gone: he was kidnapped; he was in the middle of a mid-life crisis and ran away—that sort of thing. Another routine that came up spontaneously was the building of the Mutual mansion. That started one night when a caller wanted to know why the president of the network was in his office at four in the morning. I said the poor guy had nowhere else to go, because the company had not even begun ground-breaking on the Mutual mansion. For about two weeks we did all sorts of stuff with the Mutual mansion. We had a contest about where to build it, and people nominated different cities. There was only one restriction on its location: it could not be anywhere in the Washington area; even Baltimore was too close. After all, if you're going to build a mansion for your boss, you'd like to make sure it's several hundred miles away from where you are. We also had people call in and, in a sort of takeoff on the Syracuse Chair, say they were different furnishings for the mansion. After a couple of weeks I got bored with the whole thing, though, so I blew up the mansion. How many times can you listen to intelligent people say stuff like "Larry, can I be the lamp? Now I want to talk about the Tet Offensive." We put it on the Ellipse, between the White House and the Washington Monument, and did all sorts of wild crowd noise and fantastic explosions. The wild part was that callers wouldn't let go of it—they'd call night after night with ideas for the Mutual mansion, and they were audibly disappointed when I told them it had been demolished in an urban-renewal project.

Another popular bit that kept an anxious nation up nights

was our continuing drama: Who shot M.R.? I can't remember exactly how it started; I think it was just a spontaneous response to the summerlong hype about Who shot J.R.? on the television series *Dallas*.

M.R., of course, stands for Marty Rubenstein (Marty occasionally vows he's going to get even with me for all this), and in our story M.R. was found wounded—thank God, not fatally—in his office, the impact of the bullet so severe that he had been sent into a near-permanent orbit in his swivel chair. For several weeks the listeners called in either with theories as to who had done the dastardly deed or with confessions of guilt. We promised to keep the mystery going until the end of the rating period. However, boredom killed the bit before the mystery could be solved.

One of the show's most popular comic routines came about because of my longtime dislike of psychics. Although you see them much less frequently now, during the sixties and early seventies they were a staple on the talk-show circuit. I have made it a policy to avoid psychics on the Mutual show—a policy that grew out of my last encounter with one in Miami.

To me, psychics are the biggest phonies in the world. They never have an answer to why they didn't predict some major event, but they love to give personal predictions to individuals: stuff like You've had some upsets in the past eighteen months, but things will be smoother now. Who on this planet hasn't had some upsets in the past eighteen months? Anyway, for some reason a local psychic ended up being booked on my show in Miami. I started off by asking her fairly skeptical questions, such as If you're tuning in to the President's wife and predicting she's going to have a toothache next week and you're a thousand miles away from her, how do you get your signal to her molar? How come it doesn't get hung up in Boca Raton?

My psychic did not take kindly to this line of inquiry. She

was getting more and more antsy, asking when we were going to go to the calls so she could start her predictions. I told her we weren't going to calls until she gave some answers to my questions. The third time I told her I wasn't ready to go to the calls yet, she walked off the show. Now, for reasons that escape me, psychic shows always get a strong response from listeners. There I was with hundreds of people trying to call in to find out about their Aunt Edna and I had no psychic. So as not to disappoint the callers, I decided that I would be the psychic for the evening. After all, I had the same qualifications to do predictions as any psychic: none.

My first caller was a woman who wanted to know something about her future.

"Hold on, I'm getting the signal," I said. "Yes, here it is: a week from Tuesday you are going to be in downtown Toledo with a guy named Phil."

"Larry, I've been married to the same man for thirty-six years. I'm a Coral Gables housewife. How am I going to end up in Toledo with a guy named Phil?"

"Trust me. It will be a purely sexual thing. You two will be in the Holiday Inn for four and a half days. No food. Just sex."

"Larry, I'm a fifty-eight-year-old married woman."

"I'm not responsible for what's in the stars."

To the next caller I said, "I see you have spent a lot of time in Upper Volta with someone named Mustafa Mobuto."

"Larry, I don't know where Upper Volta is and I don't know anyone named Mustafa Mobuto."

"Then you'll find out where Upper Volta is and end up there with Mustafa Mobuto."

I did all the psychic cop-outs. It was a great night.

After I started at Mutual, I told Herb Cohen, my best friend and author of *You Can Negotiate Anything*, about that incident one night over dinner. Herb was the scheduled guest that night—he was supposed to analyze the Camp David accords.

As we were talking, we both got a sort of flash that it would be fun to do a psychic spoof together. Over the rest of dinner we worked out a whole routine. Herb was to be a creature called Gork, from the planet Fringus. The greatest advantage of Fringus is that it is thirty-one days ahead of Earth, so everyone on Fringus knows a month in advance what's going to happen here. When we got back to the studio, we got the engineer to hook up a device that would distort Herb's voice so that he really would sound like a creature from another planet.

First we did an hour of absolutely straight interview on the Camp David accords. Then I thanked Herb and said good night to him. When we came back from the news, I said that I had the rare pleasure of introducing a guest who was really out of this world. If we were able to establish contact, my second guest for the evening was going to be Gork, from the planet Fringus, and Gork was going to tell us all what was in store for the next thirty-one days on Earth.

"Gork, Gork—can you hear me, Gork?" I called to Herb, who was sitting about three feet from me.

Suddenly the studio was filled with eerie, shortwave-radio-type sounds. Herb's voice, highly distorted and faraway-sounding, gradually started to come in.

"Larry, Larry, this is Gork—can you hear me, Larry?" he said. He sounded like an intergalactic Donald Duck with a Brooklyn accent. The engineers had done a great job creating a science-fiction atmosphere.

First I asked Gork to make some predictions—a simple thing for him to do since he was thirty-one days ahead of Earth. Following in the great psychic tradition, he made some daring ones:

"Larry, I can promise you that Seattle will have lots of rain, Houston will be humid this summer and the Gobi Desert will enjoy many sunny days. I predict that Delta Airlines will fly to Atlanta, and on the scientific front, a study is soon to be released that shows if your parents didn't have children, you won't either. There will be a near-tragedy in the sports world as several top tennis players will be struck with complications from what will come to be known as the Billboard Effect. The Billboard Effect describes what happens when players cover every part of their anatomy with products from sporting-good manufacturers. As a matter of fact, Jimmy Connors will be rushed to the hospital from a major tournament suffering from partial epidermis asphyxiation; that is, he will have almost endorsed himself to death."

Then I asked Gork to describe life on Fringus. From what he said, I don't think it will replace Niagara Falls as a tourist attraction.

"There's not too much to say about Fringus," Gork explained. "The most important thing to know is that it's loaded with dirt. All our meals are composed of dirt, pebbles and rocks. When we bathe, we rub mud on ourselves, and we don't have homes, we just sleep on rocks."

"That sounds grim," I said. "What do you do for pleasure?"

"Our only entertainment is watching Earth. As a matter of fact, I took a trip to Earth once."

"What were your favorite places?"

"The Rockies; Boulder, Colorado; and Pebble Beach. I felt at home there. Also, the other thing we do for fun is hang around with our soft guys."

"Soft guys?"

"Larry, on Fringus, we do not have males and females—we have hard guys and soft guys. Shirley's my soft guy—which leads me to a philosophical question: Why is it when you sit for an hour with a soft guy it seems like a minute—and when you sit on a hot, pointed rock for a second, it seems like an hour?"

"Maybe some of our listeners can help you with that one. Do you have any other questions of a philosophical nature?" I asked.

"Well, I have a few questions about Earth: Why won't Bill Bailey come home? If George Washington slept so many places, how come he never told a lie? And why is it that Howard Hughes had to die in order to prove he wasn't already dead?"

As you can tell, Gork wasn't a mere novelty on the show—he was deep. The weird thing was that my lifelong friend Herb was sitting in the studio with me, and damned if I didn't start believing he really was Gork from Fringus. When I addressed a question to him, I found myself looking up toward the heavens, or at least the ceiling, as if he could hear me better that way. The only reason I wasn't embarrassed about it was that when Herb answered, he looked down in order to direct his remarks Earthward.

The callers loved him. One woman wanted to know what flying saucers were. "They're saucers. We don't have any water on Fringus, so when we eat off a dish and it gets dirty, we just fling it into space, and some of them get to Earth."

Herb also did the usual psychic cop-outs. If an older-sounding person called, he'd always start with "You've recently been experiencing some medical troubles," which is a pretty safe bet with old people.

People were so fascinated with Fringus that somehow Gork ended up offering to send anyone who wrote in to me a sample of the soil from Fringus. We were inundated with requests. We ended up sending everyone who wrote a little sample of those Styrofoam chips used to pack fragile objects.

Gork was a hit, no question about it. For weeks afterward callers wanted to know when Gork was going to return. Probably his greatest tribute came when Herb went back home to Chicago the day after the show and asked his 12-year-old son, Richard, how he had liked it. "Oh, you were okay, Dad, but after you left, Larry had this guy Gork on who was really funny."

"What do you mean, this guy Gork?" Herb said. "*I'm* Gork."

"Come on, Dad, this guy was *really* funny."

The demand was so great that we've had Gork on several times since. Once I had former astronaut, now Senator, Harrison Schmidt call in and tell Gork that he remembered him from his own space travels.

The only uncomfortable moment we've had with Gork came when one woman called to ask him a serious question. Now, 95 percent of the callers are great when we do something like Gork; they get right into the spirit of it; but 5 percent don't get it—either they don't understand the humor, or they think I have really contacted a being from outer space. This particular woman called and said, "Larry, my daughter is very sick—I want to know what Gork says will happen to her." Your heart just sinks when something like that happens. I told her that this wasn't serious—Gork really could not predict things. "I know, but I just want to hear what he has to say." I told her it wouldn't be fair to her or to Gork to do that. But it was a powerful demonstration of how people in distress can get ripped off by charlatans.

A LOT HAS BEEN MADE of my not preparing for the show. What is being referred to is the fact that if I have an author on I don't read his or her book, or if the guest is a political figure, I don't go back over the newspaper clips on the person, or if it's a scientist, I don't do any boning up on his or her specialty.

I would not advocate my style to someone just starting out in the business—but it is something that I lucked into and that has worked for me over the years. When I started out doing my first interviews, I had no idea from day to day who the guest would be. I did the show out of a popular Miami Beach restaurant, and whoever dropped by was the person I interviewed. From that I learned never to allow any dead air; I could always think of something to keep the conversation going. Beyond that, I learned to really listen, and found that not being prepared for a guest wasn't necessarily a deficiency: it put me in the role of the audience; I learned about the subject at hand along with them. And not being prepared allowed me to ask "naive" or "obvious" questions—questions someone with some familiarity with the subject might not ask, but which a listener might want answered.

This is not to say I come to my job as a tabula rasa. I read *The Washington Post* and *The New York Times* daily, as well as the New York *Daily News*—mostly, I admit, for nostalgic reasons—and I read one out-of-town newspaper to get another perspective on events. I also read the weekly newsmagazines and alternate between fiction and nonfiction in my book reading. So I have a good working knowledge of the political and social questions of the day.

In contrast to most, if not all, of the national talk shows, I do not get a prepared list of questions from my staff, nor do they flash cue cards at me to remind me of topics to mention, nor do my guests get a pre-interview, so that a staffer can find out if the guest has any good anecdotes I should be sure to remind him of.

When the guest comes to the studio about a half-hour before the show, I make it a policy not to meet him. When we go on the air together I want it to be as spontaneous as possible. And when we go on the air, it's my baby, and I have to take responsibility for the quality of the interview.

Obviously, I miss things. I know there are occasions when the guest may have done something in 1957 that I don't know about which might be important to bring up. What is gained, however, by my method is greater than what is lost. My lack of preparation really forces me to learn, and to listen. Many interviewers are so overprepared that they forget to hear what is being said to them during the interview, and they are afraid to follow up on anything that emerges spontaneously because that might throw them off the schedule of questions so carefully prepared by the staff.

For example, I remember once watching Tom Brokaw interview Barry Goldwater on the *Today* show. Brokaw asked a few questions about whatever issue was in the news, and part of Goldwater's answer after one of the questions was "I liked Richard Nixon and I disliked him. I had mixed feelings about him all along until one day in the White House about a week before the resignation. That was the final straw." What did Brokaw do? He went on to the next question on his list, never bothering to ask what in the world it was Richard Nixon did that made Barry Goldwater give up on him.

Of course, on the *Today* show the purpose is to get the political figure in question to make x number of statements on the topic at hand in the course of about four minutes. That precludes the kind of in-depth interview I try to do. And unlike the *Today* show, which tries to make news with its interviews, I aim for a feature interview. That is, I want my listeners to end up knowing everything they can about my guest and the topic he may be discussing. I feel I am a conduit for the audience' questions, so I am careful to try not to intrude myself or my beliefs into the interview; that's fine for "Open Phone"— that's what "Open Phone" is all about—but during the interview the person being exposed should be the guest.

I operate the same way during the portion of the show in which the guest takes calls—I'm there to move the calls along, not become part of the dialogue. One of the advantages of having callers when you work as I do is that if I do miss some significant point in the interview, particularly a point the guest may not necessarily volunteer himself, you can be sure that there will be no lack of callers ready to bring it up.

The callers are an absolutely vital part of the show, but call-in shows work only if the host keeps a firm grip on the proceedings. I admit I can be brusque, although I am careful not to resort to rudeness, but it would be irresponsible of me to allow callers to linger for fear of offending. One person may be having a lovely conversation while millions of listeners are being bored to tears. I think callers have come to respect the fact that I'll force them to get to the point. (After all, we have no 800 number, so I'm saving the callers some money by keeping their questions short.) For example, if the guest is a doctor and a caller comes on and says, "About eleven years ago I started to get this pain . . ." I'll immediately force the person to state his question. The question itself may be a very good one, such as Why are back problems so hard to treat?, so I get the caller to say that, instead of giving his medical history, which no one wants to hear.

A good host also must be able to go with his instincts—or more important, have instincts. I remember once on "Open Phone" a woman called in to say that she was a big fan of the show; she got a lot of current-affairs information from it. She added that she was blind, so that radio shows were a real lifeline for her. As I talked with her, she mentioned that one of her hobbies was bowling.

Now, most people when confronted with a handicapped person are both uncomfortable and curious. But instead of being able to deal with the handicap straightforwardly, they pretend it doesn't exist, and then scurry off so they won't have to deal with their own discomfort at confronting a handicap. I've had many handicapped people on my show, both as guests on specifically to discuss handicaps and as guests on to discuss other topics who happened to be handicapped. I don't want to say people with various disabilities are any more alike than any other group, but I have found that most of them are perfectly straightforward about their handicap, and being able to discuss it straightforwardly has the wonderful effect of banishing all discomfort.

That is a long way of saying that a sighted person would immediately wonder how someone who is blind bowls. So I said to her, "How do you bowl if you're blind?" She told me that she had 5-percent vision, enough to be able to bowl. There was no offense given or taken in our exchange; and I think listeners learned something about not automatically assuming a handicapped person can't participate in so-called "normal" activities.

Not every talk-show host works as I do, of course. Here are my opinions of some of my colleagues:

CAVETT: Cavett is a conversationalist—he is as much the subject of the interview as the guest. But this works for Cavett because he's clever and witty and gives listeners the sense that they are the third person at a dinner party. Cavett presumes a certain familiarity with the subject, however. If he has a ballet dancer on, you'll get much more out of the interview if you know something about ballet. If I interview a ballet dancer, you don't have to know anything about it; I'll make sure all the basic questions are answered.

CARSON: Carson is great. He knows exactly what works for him, and he sticks with it. He wants his guests to be good, and he plays off the guest to his and the guest's advantage. Carson, however, is an entertainer; he is not there to provide information. Ideally, a talk show should entertain and inform, but Carson does the entertaining so well that the rest doesn't matter.

LETTERMAN: I think David Letterman is wonderful although I've seen the show only on vacations because of the time conflict. Letterman is a true comic talent, but as a serious interviewer he seems hesitant and uncomfortable. I see him as more of a young Ernie Kovacs than as a traditional talk-show host. If I were the producer, I'd drop the pretext of doing serious interviews and make everything comic.

SNYDER: Tom Snyder is a noninterviewer. He's out there interviewing himself. This is not to say he's not a very nice guy; he is.

And it is also not to say that what he does is unsatisfactory. A lot of people are interested in a dollop of Tom Snyder on Tom Snyder.

DOUGLAS: Mike Douglas is an affable former band singer who in all the years he's been on the air has never developed a personality as an interviewer. One senses his questions come right off the TelePrompTer.

HARTMAN: David Hartman got a lot of flak when he started on *Good Morning America* because he was an actor, not a newsman. However, I think he's proved that he's very good at what he does. He's not going to break any new ground, but he'll get the job done. An important part of his success is that he is perfect for that particular show. He wears very well, and you want someone who is easy to take at that hour of the morning.

DONAHUE: Donahue is an excellent issue-oriented interviewer who has developed a style that is perfect for him. He plays devil's advocate superbly, and he knows how to work an audience.

GRIFFIN: Griffin was a much better interviewer ten years ago than he is now. He used to have a nice combination of an innocent curiosity and a wry sense of the absurd. In the past few years, however, I think he has come to rely too much on a steady stream of show-biz chitchat. He doesn't have that pleasing, slightly skeptical edge he once had.

WALTERS: Barbara Walters has done some very good interviews, particularly hard-news interviews. I think her mistake has been to turn herself into an intellectual Rona Barrett by doing useless interviews with vapid celebrities. She has also become quite affected—her breathless earnestness over what some TV actress has to say. In addition, she has the problem of having become more famous than her guests, which is a bad situation for an interviewer to get into.

I remember Walter Cronkite telling a story about going to cover some caucus at one of the presidential nominating conventions. As soon as Cronkite entered the room, the caucus stopped its business while everyone lined up to get his autograph. Though being famous is a bigger problem for a newsman than for an interviewer, it's important for an interviewer not to become a captive of his own celebrity. That is, not to lose sight of the fact that the reason he became famous is that he is good at what he does. It is easy to grow soft when you constantly get rewarded for being famous, not for being good.

Because I'm not on television, the open door to fame, my celebrityhood is of a very low-key sort. When you don't have an immediately recognizable face, you get to live a fairly normal life. Part of my problem in Miami was that even though I knew I was no better than anybody else, because I was so well known people deferred to me as if I were. No matter how mature you are—and I wasn't at all—it's hard not to let that go to your head. The occasions on which I am recognized now by listeners are so few that they are pleasant, not intrusive.

Once in New York a couple of years ago I went into a drugstore to buy a pack of razor blades. The pharmacist was behind the counter with his back to me arranging the stock, and I asked him for the brand of blade. Without turning around, he said, "Stop, I know you; you can't fool me." He then turned and called to his wife, who was in back of the store, "Come out here—you won't believe who's here." His wife came out, and as he handed me the blades, he said, "Larry King. You think I wouldn't recognize that voice? I listen to you all the time."

A similar incident happened when I was in Chicago for the Bar Mitzvah of one of Herb's sons. We were all at a restaurant having dinner. When I gave my order to the waiter, a woman at the next table jumped up and came over. "I'd know that voice anywhere," she said. "Where's Mr. Rubenstein?"

And if ever I am tempted to let this go to my head, I can always talk to one of the other Larry Kings and know that some of my biggest fans aren't too sure who I am. The other Larry Kings are Larry L. King, journalist and playwright, author of *The Best Little Whorehouse in Texas*, and Larry King, businessman and husband of Billie Jean King. Our lovers, barbers and editors get the three of us confused.

I have had both of them on the show, and there is no end of stories we can tell about mistaken identity and misdelivered mail. My show was first picked up in New York City at the same time that playwright King's *Best Little Whorehouse* was opening there. Both of us had articles about us in the New York papers, and after a story about me appeared, a social-ite/writer/former girlfriend of Larry L.'s whom he hadn't spo-ken to in two years called him up and congratulated him on his success and said she wanted to come on his show. Larry L. didn't quite understand: as far as he knew, his former girlfriend was not a singer, dancer or actress. "I'm terribly sorry," he told her, "all the parts are filled." "What do you mean, all the parts are filled?" she replied. "I want to be on your radio show."

Larry L. told me that he has stopped trying to convince his barber he doesn't host a late-night radio show. He simply sits in the barber chair and listens to critiques of the show while he gets his hair cut.

Once, Larry L. wrote a commissioned piece—a commis-sioned piece—for *Washingtonian* magazine. The cutline de-scribed him as the author of *Best Little Whorehouse* and host of my radio show.

I get my share of this mistaken identity as well. Once about 3 or 4 A.M. on "Open Phone" a guy called up and said to me, "Larry, I've never liked you. I don't agree with your politics, I don't like most of your guests, but in the past week or so I've come to admire you."

I couldn't think of anything I'd done in the past week to change anybody's opinion of me, so I asked him why he felt different about me.

"I think you've shown great sensitivity toward your wife, and I admire you for it," he said. "I don't know what I'd do if I found out my wife was a lesbian."

"Listen, as I look back on it, I have to say part of it was my fault. I just spent too much time wrapped up in the show."

"Larry, I wouldn't feel guilty if I were you; you just can never totally know someone even if you're married to her."

"Yeah, but I keep wondering whether or not there was something I should have done."

"I don't know. But you've done the right thing by sticking by her," he said.

Talk about not being able to help yourself. I could tell this guy was absolutely sincere and he was convinced I was married to Billie Jean King. The rest of the night all the callers ribbed me mercilessly about that one.

ALTHOUGH WE DON'T TRY to create news the way *Today* or *Good Morning America* tries to, the great thing about being live is that when a story breaks between midnight and dawn, we've got a good chance of being the first network show to get hold of it.

For example, we broke the ending of the baseball strike, although I have to admit that a little proprietary interest was part of that scoop. What happened was that the various parties reached a settlement at about 2:45 A.M. EST. The president of the American League, Lee McPhail, called California Angels owner Gene Autry to alert him and tell him to get the word out to the other owners. Autry did not get to be the success he is by neglecting his own interests. Before he told any of the other owners, he called his own radio-station group, Golden West Broadcasting, and told them. Four of those five stations happened to run *The Larry King Show*—so they alerted us to the end of the strike, and at 3:05 we got Gene Autry on the phone and broke the story nationally. However, although the players and owners had reached a basic agreement, they hadn't

yet announced that fact to the reporters camped at the door of
the negotiating room because they were still working out the
details. Some of the reporters happened to be listening to my
show that morning and learned that the strike had been settled
under their noses. They were not pleased that after their long
vigil they weren't given the news first. I was told they stormed
into the negotiating room and demanded to be told what had
happened.

Two other news stories we got a crack at both concerned
the Iranian hostage situation. The first was the morning of
the failed rescue attempt. From that experience I really
have to admire the reporters, particularly broadcasters, who
have to cover sudden, dramatic stories. There is an adren-
aline high at feeling you are right there on top of the event.
But it is not easy to make sense of a situation that is changing
from moment to moment and about which you have had no
warning.

When we got the bulletin that several Americans had died
in a hostage-rescue attempt, we immediately turned the show
over to the story. The evening's guest had left by that time, but
in between updates from Mutual reporters we managed to get
hold of Clement Zablocki, the chairman of the House Foreign
Relations Committee. Someone on the staff also woke up Senator Henry Jackson, who drove out to the studio and came on
the show to take calls and discuss the situation. He was furious
that he hadn't been informed by President Carter that a rescue
attempt was going to take place. The overwhelming majority
of the calls about the attempt were favorable; people felt it was
good that we had at least tried something. It wasn't until the
next day or so that the impact of yet another failure sank in.
And the unspeakable treatment by the Iranians of the bodies
of the American soldiers only deepened the callers' sense of
impotence and rage.

During that period we also did a show with two Iranians,

one pro-Shah, one pro-Khomeini. The pro-Shah Iranian was a man named Ali Tabatabai who had become active in the attempt to return the monarchy to Iran. He came escorted by several bodyguards and talked obsessively about how the revolutionaries were out to kill him. I remember thinking at the time that he was the most paranoid person I had ever met. A few months later, Ali Tabatabai was killed at the front door of his suburban Washington home by the people he had said were out to get him.

The other occasion with the hostages was less dramatic, but was quite a coup for my resourceful staff. The hostage release was the biggest story of the day—getting as much press as the first days of the Reagan Administration. When the fifty-one Americans finally got back to this country, they were virtually quarantined from the press. Naturally, the media were crazy to get hold of a hostage, any hostage, for a firsthand account of their ordeal.

After a stop with their families at West Point, the hostages were flown to Washington for a heroes' welcome in the city. Still under tight security, they were put up at the Marriott in Crystal City, Virginia, just over the bridge from D.C., and coincidentally the building next to the Mutual Broadcasting studios, home of you know who. There we were, a few hundred feet from the hottest story in the country, and we couldn't get to it. Our staff went over to stake out the Marriott, with no better luck than the dozens of other reporters there. We had finally conceded that we would have to go with our regular guest that night when someone came up to the studio and said that several of the hostages had been spotted in the disco in the basement of our building. I must digress here to give a word about our location. Although we are not in Washington, D.C., proper, Crystal City is about ten minutes outside the District and is one of those enormous complexes that ring the city and which appear to grow an average of an office building a week.

Our building is a sort of Alice in Wonderland affair with restaurants, shops and a disco in the basement. To get to an office
upstairs, however, you really have to know where you're going,
as the building is laid out with no discernible logic. This is
doubly true at night, when Security locks the upper floors and
to get to our studio a guest has to locate a building telephone
and have Security clear the elevator to our floor. Staffers have
had to make many a late-night foray through the building
looking for lost guests. Guests have been found in the garage,
the disco and miscellaneous hallways. One guest ended up
opening a fire door which triggered an alarm. He claimed it
was an accident; we have always believed he did it out of desperation.

In any case, the night of the hostage release we were grateful
our building is like a small city, in that we figured if we had
hostages in the disco, we might be able to persuade them to
come to the studio.

Down went then-producer Jack Kirby and then–studio
director Laurie Fineran. Since reports were that the dancing
hostages were all Marines, we figured Laurie would make a
more persuasive case for the show than Jack. It wasn't too hard
to spot the Marines, and sure enough, with about ten minutes
until air time, Laurie had homed in on one. He was Sergeant
John McKeel from Texas. Although he was in excellent spirits,
he was reluctant to do the show, since the government had decided the hostages weren't free enough to decide whether or
not they wanted to talk to the press. Finally, Jack and Laurie
persuaded him to come upstairs for a cup of coffee. If he decided he wanted to go on, he could; if not, he was welcome to
sit in the studio and watch the show. Just as the midnight news
was ending, and our scheduled guest was standing by, McKeel
said what the hell, and decided to do the show. He stayed for
two hours and told in fascinating detail about his experiences—including how the hostages communicated by writing

notes to each other on toilet paper, and the fact that they had decided to escape if release did not come soon.

WHEN MIDNIGHT ROLLS AROUND, I am, as they say in broadcasting, solely responsible for the content of *The Larry King Show*. But there would be no *Larry King Show* without five other people: Marty Rubenstein, president of the network; Tom O'Brien, executive producer of the show; Tammy Haddad, producer; Colleen Moran, studio director, and Mary Tydings, who handles the administrative end of the show. These are the people who make sure that when midnight does roll around I have an interview to conduct, and that once it is under way everything runs smoothly.

Tom O'Brien, who came to Mutual from ABC News with Marty Rubenstein, oversees the whole show—handles the budget, approves the selection of guests. Tammy Haddad runs the show's day-to-day operations and books the guests. Colleen Moran handles the phone calls and makes sure everything is in order during the broadcast, and Mary Tydings makes sure our office isn't paralyzed in a blizzard of paper. I have just about no administrative skills, so these people make it possible for there to be a *Larry King Show*. And while I can suggest guests or veto them, I exercise that right rarely. I trust Tammy and Tom to come up with people who will interest me and the audience.

One unusual and highly satisfying aspect of my relationship with Mutual is the trust management has shown in me. The show works, and they are happy to let it keep working. I am never bothered with memos asking why I said this or didn't say that. I have to admit that, in part, this freedom is due to the fact that I work in the middle of the night. It helps to make up for the fact that I am perpetually out of sync with most of the world.

Because our technical and personnel needs are so minimal, we've been able to take the show on the road quite a bit. Two of our most interesting times on location were at the 1980 Republican and Democratic conventions.

I am a lifelong Democrat, and 1980 was not a good year for my party. It's not that I want to kick sand in the Democrats' faces, but I have to admit that our experience at their convention was made notable by its screw-ups. The major one was the night that Representative Morris Udall was booked as our main guest. Udall was the keynote speaker at the convention, and he was scheduled for the show on the convention's first night. Now, the security at Madison Square Garden was tighter than that at Fort Knox. You had to have about sixteen different passes to get access to sixteen different parts of the hall. I think you even had to have a bathroom pass. No one was taking any chances at this convention, believe me. The night Udall was to appear, the convention session broke up around 11 P.M., so Udall decided to go back to his hotel nearby and have a bite to eat and freshen up and come back to the Garden to do our show. He sauntered back to the Garden about ten minutes before we went on the air and showed his credentials to the guard so he could get back in. The guard looked at the credentials and said, "Sorry, I can't let you in there." He went on to say that once you left the hall at night your credentials expired and you needed a whole new set to get back in. Udall protested that he was scheduled to appear on my show in five minutes. The guard said that made no difference to him, Udall wasn't getting back into the hall. Then Udall decided to pull rank and told the guard that he was a congressman, the keynote speaker for the convention, and he had to get back into the Garden. The guard told him he knew exactly who he was, as a matter of fact he recognized Udall from television, but he wasn't getting through the door. Disgusted, Udall went around the block to another exit, figuring he had just run into an overzealous guard. At the next entrance, however, the situation was exactly the same—the guard even complimented him on his speech while refusing him entry. So Udall decided to try the next exit.

By this time, of course, we were moments from going on the air. Someone from the staff called Udall's hotel room to find out where in the world he was. His wife answered and said with some concern that he had left several minutes ago and that he should have gotten to the studio by now. Udall or no Udall, we had to go on the air—so I opened with an all-points bulletin asking anyone with information on the whereabouts of Representative Morris Udall to contact *The Larry King Show*.

Udall never made it; after his fourth unsuccessful try at entry, he gave up and went back to the hotel. When it was clear Mo Udall was at large somewhere in New York and wasn't going to make it, our staffers went scouring the Garden, and someone corralled Chip Carter to pinch-hit for Udall. The funny thing about the security is that my friend Herb Cohen managed to breach the security system. Herb had only a peripheral pass, which allowed him access to the stands, but not the convention floor. Herb decided he wanted to be where the action was, so on the way down to the floor he stopped a guard, quickly flashed his credentials, patted the guard on the back and said, "You're doing a great job" and walked onto the floor. The poor guard just waved Herb along, figuring he must be some kind of Garden official.

The wildest night of the convention trips was the night we had Gerald Ford booked on the show. Mutual rented a yacht and docked it right near the Republican convention site in Detroit, and we set up a studio on it. Anytime you have a former President go anywhere, you are inundated with Secret Service agents; this night was no exception. But what made Ford's appearance unusual was that he was booked on what turned out to be the night of the wild, and ultimately unsuccessful, negotiations to get Ford to be Ronald Reagan's running mate. When we scheduled Ford, weeks in advance, we had no idea he would be quite the hot property he became. But as the night progressed, and the television speculation grew more feverish and everyone was going crazy trying to figure out what Ford and Reagan were going to do, our show became quite a center of attention. Someone from our show called Ford's people about every half-hour as the night went on just to make sure he was still going to come, and his people kept saying we were still on Ford's schedule. You must remember that no one in the media had any access to Ford or Reagan during all the hours the speculation was going on, so when word got out that the former President was going to appear on our show at midnight, all hell broke loose. We had camera crews and reporters crawling all over the place; Secret Service agents were swarming aboard the boat; frogmen were checking under the boat for explosives; helicopters were monitoring the scene from above; and hundreds of spectators were waiting for a glimpse of anyone who might show up.

Finally, around 11:30, word came that the deal had fallen through and that the vice-presidential nomination was going to George Bush. Things had gotten so wild that Reagan made an unusual appearance at the hall to tell people it wasn't going to be a Reagan-Ford ticket. By this time staffers were calling Ford's people every ten minutes; we couldn't believe we were going to get a scoop on the biggest news story of the convention. Yes, they kept assuring us, Mr. Ford was still coming.

When it comes to doing the show I almost always feel cool and in control, but this night I started to get rattled. At 11:45 Ford was still scheduled to come, at 11:50 Ford was still scheduled to come, and at 11:55, five minutes before we go on the air, Ford's people called: Ford wasn't coming. They were very nice about it: they explained that after everything that had gone on this should really be Ronald Reagan and George

Bush's night; Ford felt that if he did an interview then it would focus too much attention on him. We did get a promise that Ford would appear the following night, however. Luckily, the comedian Mark Russell was standing by, so he came on and did his analysis of why a Reagan-Ford ticket wouldn't work: "It would have been terrible. How would you have addressed them? Mr. Vice President and Mr. President? Mr. President and Mr. President? Mr. President and Mr. former President currently Vice President?" Then he explained that the real reason Ford couldn't come that night was that he had bumped his head while he was closing on a condo in Vail.

The next night, as promised, Ford did show up, along with the frogmen, the helicopters, the TV cameras and the spectators.

There we were, Ford surrounded by security men, people jammed around the boat trying to get a look. My first question to him was "Well, what brings you to town?"

"I'm a Michigan boy, Larry, and Betty and I like to come back every so often and visit old friends," he said.

Ford was a marvelous guest: open and down-to-earth. He was very straightforward about the negotiations, not coy and bombastic as so many politicians can be when talking about something that might be uncomfortable. He said that he really had been interested in being on the ticket, but from previous experience he knew how tough it was to be Vice President.

"There are no specific duties for the Vice President spelled out in the Constitution except presiding over the Senate," he said. "When I selected Nelson Rockefeller to be my Vice President, I told him, 'Nelson, it's going to be different with us— you'll be my right arm.' In six months I forgot his name, and Nelson was one of the brightest men in politics. It wasn't his fault; it's the fault of the system.

"What I was trying to say to Reagan was not that I expected to be co-President, but that I wanted some specific areas that would be in my domain, and decision-making abilities over these areas, like that of a corporate vice president. But Reagan couldn't guarantee that. And he was right: you can't guarantee that."

Most of the calls, obviously, were about how he felt at possibly becoming Vice President again, what did he think of the ticket, that sort of thing. There is no pretention to Jerry Ford, and most of the callers addressed this former President without awe. His first caller was a housewife from Topeka. Although I force my callers to get to their questions immediately, I could tell right away that this woman from Topeka was going to have trouble getting to her point; but in another way, she made the most eloquent of points concerning the show.

"I've been watching the television the past few days, and after all that's happened I can't believe that now I'm talking to you," she said.

That's really what the show offers: a chance for people from all over the country to put their questions directly, as equals, to our guests. And often, it is the guest who ends up getting the most out of the experience.

One of the most touching nights on the show occurred just because of this interaction between guest and callers. In September of 1980, Danny Kaye was in Washington on business involving UNICEF and we booked him for the show. In order to get Danny, we had to agree to have a UNICEF official on for a half-hour as well. Danny, the UNICEF guy and Danny's brother—a retired businessman visiting from Miami—all came to the studio at the appointed hour. Danny asked how long he was scheduled for, and he was told it was an hour of interview, then two hours of calls. Kaye was taken aback—no way he would stay three hours; forget it. He said he would stay until 1 A.M. By this time it was 11:45, and at that hour it's exceedingly difficult to get another guest to agree to pinch-hit. What could we do? We had to go along with what Kaye said.

The first part, with the UNICEF guy, was all right, if predictable. After he left I started talking to Danny about his career, growing up in Brooklyn, his many interests outside of show business. Things were going well, so Danny agreed to stay a little bit after 1 and take calls. It was in that part of the show that the real magic took over. There was an absolute outpouring of love for Danny over the phone. There were many good questions, but a lot of people just called to say how much pleasure he had brought them over the years. Danny was stunned by the whole thing.

The highlight came when a woman called and said, "Danny, as I'm talking to you, I'm looking at a picture of you that's sitting on the mantelpiece next to a picture of my son. My son was killed in Korea, and he was your biggest fan. In his footlocker where most boys put a picture of some starlet, he had a picture of you. They sent that picture home with him, and I put it up there on the mantelpiece."

At that point the woman started to cry, Danny started to cry and his brother began to cry. I was close to tears myself. Then Danny said to her, "What song of mine did your son like best?" The woman told him one of her son's favorites, and Danny sang it to her over the phone. I'm sure I wasn't the only person listening who had goose bumps.

Kaye also did a wonderful, very human thing with the callers. He made sure he had a question for each of them: What did they do for a living? How come they were up listening?—that sort of thing. It was lovely of him to do that. At one point we started talking about his growing up in Brooklyn. To every Brooklyn kid Danny Kaye was a legend. He was expelled from three high schools, and he finally left school for good at about 16. He was known as a crazy kid—he'd imitate Tarzan in class, throw ink, disrupt gym class. He said, "You see, I've never changed. I went into my craziness. I was crazy in school and they threw me out because of it, but I found out that if you stand up on a stage and act crazy, people will pay you for it."

The hours just flew by, and at 3 A.M., when we got to "Open Phone," I thanked Danny for being such a marvelous guest.

"That's it—it's over?" he asked.

I explained to him that at three o'clock the guest left and I took calls on any subject.

"Okay, I'll stay for that," he said.

What happens with the show is that on the West Coast, because of the time difference, the listeners get "Open Phone America" first and then, after I've signed off in Washington, the stations run a tape of the first three hours. When we came back on after the news at ten past three, Danny welcomed the West Coast and then did a recap of the preceding three hours so that listeners there would not feel left out. He then took calls until five-thirty in the morning.

WHEN YOU HAVE a great name in the field of entertainment, you always get a lot of adoring calls. Bob Hope, who's been on the show four times, is no exception. But something unexpected happened with Hope: he got hostile calls as well. Hope was shocked by them—he's not used to anything but love. You could see how startled he was by the look on his face. There were not all that many negative calls, but the ones that came were all along the same lines: either direct criticism of his support of the Vietnam war, or questioning of his altruism because he was paid for the shows he did for the troops and got a lot of publicity when they were broadcast.

Hope got immediately defensive. He said that most of the shows he did for the troops never were broadcast, and half of all the work he does is charitable.

Hope is a difficult interview. What you see is exactly what you get. He has his jokes and his patter, and he is quite uncomfortable when he is forced to break out of a structured situation, or is asked to be introspective. I asked him a few questions about the life of a professional comedian: whether he has absolute faith in his ability to make an audience laugh; what does it feel like to be able to control the reactions of huge numbers of people. He said, "I've been doing it so long that I'm used to it." That is not the sort of answer that makes for an easy interview.

What was most telling about Hope was his response to the many calls he got from his adoring fans, people who had seen him perform in their hometowns twenty, even thirty years ago. He had an absolutely uncanny memory when it came to his career. One woman called and told him she remembered him performing at some theater in Cleveland years ago, and he said, "Oh, yes, that's the one where the doormen wear those funny hats."

The almost obsessive concern with their careers, the need for constant feedback is a fairly common character trait even in the most successful performers. I remember Milton Berle telling a real show-business joke. It seems a nightclub comic is in his dressing room when he hears a knock on the door; he opens it and in walks an absoluteoly gorgeous woman. She says to him, "I think you're the funniest man in the world. I think you're one of the greatest performers I've ever seen." As she's saying this she starts taking off her clothes. With each garment she tells the comic how brilliant he is, how much he makes her laugh. Finally, the woman is naked, and she lies down on the floor and says to him, "I'm yours. Do anything you want to me. I want to make love to the most brilliant comedian in the world." The comic looks at this beautiful woman there on the floor waiting for him and says to her, "Which show did you catch?"

Berle said that joke was so true because the need for adulation and reassurance is what attracts so many performers to the business in the first place.

Berle's insight into the show-biz mentality does not, however, exempt him from being subject to it himself. Even in his 70s he has a constant need to perform, to be noticed. And he's still raucously funny. I had him on when we were doing the show from Las Vegas and he was as wild as he ever was in his heyday. But it also came through loud and clear that he misses being the center of attention. And center of attention he was. During the fifties the streets were deserted on Tuesday nights when his show was broadcast. People bought television sets just to see Milton Berle. When you went in to buy a set, you always checked the channel his show was on before you took it home: the most important thing about it was that it got good reception for the Milton Berle show. In my neighborhood Herb was the first kid whose family owned a television set, and twenty of us would go over to his house on Tuesdays just to see Uncle Miltie.

Berle had a unique thirty-year contract with NBC that just expired in 1981. Of course, the network had stopped using him as a performer years before it ran out; NBC paid him then to be a "consultant." During our interview he made no bones about his bitterness at the fact that he was a consultant in name only. He felt he still had a lot to offer.

Berle is very much in the mold of a host of Jewish comedians who made their way out of poverty to become big stars. They are brash, egotistical, yet charming, as is demonstrated in Berle's answer to a question I asked him about his reputation as a ladies' man.

"It's all true," he said. "I have really lived the life people fantasized Sinatra had."

You can still see it today. Berle had lunch with Sharon and me. I might as well not have existed. He wasn't obnoxious about it—most of the conversation was Berle giving Sharon advice on how to handle my finances—but there was definitely some flirtation going on there.

The calls Berle got were almost all of an adoring nature.

There were a lot of nostalgia calls as well; people reminiscing about the early years of television, recalling bits that Berle did. Berle ate it up. However, I remember one question that really set him off: a caller wanted to know why so many top comedians are Jewish. That's a legitimate question, but Berle got very defensive. He took the question to mean that he was funny *because* he was Jewish. He said being Jewish had nothing to do with it—he was funny because he was funny.

VERY FEW TALK SHOWS suffer from a lack of available authors. *The Larry King Show* has its share of writers, although we try to keep them to no more than 30 percent of the guests. Lots of talk-show hosts complain about authors: all they want to do is hawk their book; they're usually so beat out from book tours that they don't have anything interesting to say. I like having authors on. First of all, we've got so much time to talk that they can usually stop worrying about making sure they tell the one little anecdote they hope makes their book sound interesting before the next guest gets on the show. Second, I like the challenge of interviewing someone who never wants to see a microphone again.

The fans of particular writers, I've discovered, are no less ardent than the fans of movie stars. Actually, a strong point of our show is that we can simultaneously satisfy a specific and a general audience. For example, when violinist Itzhak Perelman was on, we got questions ranging from how does he get a particular sound out of a particular passage in a Beethoven sonata to what is the best way to go about learning something about classical music. It's the same way with authors. Callers range from people who have read every word of the writer to someone whose interest was just piqued from something he heard on the show.

Joseph Heller was someone who got a lot of reverential calls. The problem was that the reverence was for his first book, *Catch-22*, while Heller was trying to sell copies of his latest book, *Good as Gold*. There were quite a few callers who expressed almost a sense of betrayal about Heller's second book, *Something Happened*, which they felt did not measure up to the standard he had set with *Catch-22*. Heller was quite candid about the difficulties of starting a writing career with a work many people consider perfect. He said part of the reason for J. D. Salinger's becoming a recluse was a reaction to similar pressure he got as a result of *Catcher in the Rye*. Heller told an anecdote about that pressure. He said that the first time Norman Mailer met John F. Kennedy, Kennedy said to him, "I just loved your novel (pause) *Deer Park.*" Whether he was sincere or just being a good politician, Mailer wanted to kiss J.F.K. All his professional life Mailer had been hearing how great his first novel, *The Naked and the Dead*, was, and how disappointing subsequent ones had been.

Rod McKuen is not someone who has ever received the critical acclaim that Joseph Heller has; nonetheless, there are people who think poetry begins and ends with Rod McKuen. McKuen, however, has no pretensions about his work. "Why should I get mad at what the critics say about me?" he said. "I've never said, 'Here's my next book of great poetry.' All I can do is hope that I reach a few people." He did say, though, that to thwart the critics he once published a volume of poems under a pseudonym. "I got some great reviews—from people who had panned my other books," he said.

McKuen said he didn't want to spend a lot of time on the show hyping his book, so he told me if he could say one thing about his book at the beginning, we wouldn't have to mention it again. "I have a new book out," he said, "and anyone who buys the book and cuts the corner flap and sends it to me will get a free copy of my last record." Clever little promotion device—or so McKuen thought. Two hundred and fifteen thousand people sent the flap. It ended up costing him a fortune in records.

THE MUTUAL BROADCASTING SYSTEM was organized in the 1930s by a group of local station owners who wanted to fight the programming stranglehold of the other networks. They decided to mutually (hence the name) fund their venture and come up with their own shows. They had something of a magic touch: their offerings included *Superman, The Lone Ranger* and *The Shadow*. They offered sports, and had their own star personalities, including Gabriel Heatter. Mutual, however, decided to stick with its strengths and not invest any money in that strange new invention, television. So while the other networks became radio-and-television giants, Mutual stayed with its original medium, and owing to that and its own management problems, it fell into hard times by the 1950s. It bounced around from owner to owner for the next couple of decades until 1977, when the Amway Corporation bought it and turned Mutual around. Mutual today is the only national network whose business is exclusively radio. The network's comeback has been substantial: it now has 950 affiliate stations and offers, in addition to my show, news, sports, life-style reports, music and special features.

Mutual's programs are made available to affiliate stations to air at their discretion. There is no charge to the affiliate for taking *The Larry King Show*; instead, Mutual gets the revenue from a percentage of the advertising spots built into the show, while the station gets to keep the revenue from the local advertisers to whom it sells the remaining air time.

For the first few years of the show, most of our selling efforts were aimed not at advertisers but at affiliate stations. That is, we have tried to induce as many stations around the country as possible to carry *The Larry King Show*, the theory being that if we get the audience hooked, the national advertisers' dollars will follow. In spite of the success of our efforts at signing up affiliates, advertisers have been reluctant to buy in. The show is in the black, but it is not the moneymaker it should be.

Two things should help change that. One, Mutual is now starting to turn its selling efforts from affiliate to advertiser. The other, ironically, is that because of our success, the other networks have been talking about having their own late-night radio shows. We welcome the competition. Why shouldn't we?—we'll be best. And moreover, competition should make us stronger. As Marty Rubenstein says, if the other networks are willing to get into the game, it will prove to the still-reluctant big advertisers that there's always a market before the dawn.

I also should acknowledge the enlightened management policies of the owners of Mutual, the Amway Corporation. They do the best thing any owners could do: they let us alone. Amway was started about twenty years ago by two Michigan businessmen, Rich DeVoss and Jay Van Andel. They have built a billion-dollar empire with their home-care products, which are sold through individual distributors, not through stores. The owners of Amway are very conservative politically. Rich DeVoss is finance chairman of the Republican National Committee; Jay was president of the U.S. Chamber of Commerce. Both of them are strong Reagan supporters. In other words, we don't agree politically on a thing. Except, that is, the right we each have to express our beliefs. Mutual's owners have never once tried to censor me or influence the selection of my guests. Rich DeVoss has appeared on the show in his capacity as an R.N.C. official—an appearance that was shortly followed with one by his Democratic counterpart.

PART III

Nice Jewish Boy

FOR YEARS, whenever I saw a police squad car I got a sick feeling in the pit of my stomach.

Saturday morning, June 10, 1944, I was carrying home a load of books from the library when I saw them: three squad cars parked in front of the apartment building. Instinctively, I ran to the front door and up the stairs to our third-floor walk-up. Before I got to the door, I heard my mother screaming. I was 10 years old, and terrified. On the landing I ran into one of the police officers, who scooped me up and carried me back downstairs and put me into the flivver. (Squad cars were called "flivvers" in my neighborhood.) We started to drive, and slowly, and with much compassion, he told me that my father had died of a heart attack. The two of us drove around most of the day. He told me I was the man of the house now and that my mother needed me to be brave. Not wanting to leave me,

97

the cop took me to the matinee at Loews Pitkin: *Bataan*, with Robert Taylor. (I interviewed Taylor twenty-five years later, and he was touched when I told him of the incident.) At about 6 P.M. the policeman took me back home. My 6-year-old brother, Marty, didn't know what was going on. "Where's Daddy?" "When's Daddy coming home?" he kept asking. By this time, cousins and aunts and uncles had arrived to try to comfort my distraught mother. I kept being told that I was the man of the house now—but I didn't know what that meant. I heard whispered talk that my brother and I would be sent to camp, which terrified me even more. I didn't go to the funeral; I was thought to be too young. I remember spending the afternoon bouncing a rubber ball on the stoop for hours. I didn't cry. I didn't feel anything except the certainty that nothing would ever be the same again.

The reason there were three cars full of cops at the house the morning my father died was simply that they were friends of his who wanted to give whatever comfort they could to his widow. My father, Eddie Zeiger, had immigrated from Russia as a boy, and like many immigrants, was a fierce patriot. He and my mother, Jennie, owned a bar-and-grill in the Brownsville section of Brooklyn called, appropriately enough, "Eddie's." It was located under the tracks of the el—the elevated train—about four blocks from our walk-up apartment. The bar-and-grill—my parents called it a store—was located on a fairly rugged corner, so there were many policemen patrolling the neighborhood, all of whom became great friends of Eddie Zeiger's. It was hard not to love my father; he was a character, a storyteller—in Yiddish, a tummler. His place was a ghetto version of Toots Shor's. My father was a passionate sports fan and racing fan; the radio was a focus of our lives—a way to keep track of those interests. Unlike his son, however, my father never let his gambling get out of control.

We were poor, but like so many people who grew up in that

environment, I didn't know it. My parents had an unusually happy marriage; in spite of being together nearly all day, they continued to enjoy each other's company. And I never felt there was anything in the world I was in need of. Because of my father's love for America—an immigrant boy grows up to own his own store: that was the American dream—he wanted to repay the country when World War II broke out. He decided to enlist in the Army, but the armed forces didn't have too great a need for men over 40. That was not enough to deter my father. He sold the store for next to nothing and took a job in a defense plant. If he couldn't serve one way, he would serve another. The plant was located in Kearny, New Jersey, and my father joined the night shift and helped build warships. On the afternoon of June 9 he complained to my mother of chest pains. She was quite concerned, since my father was not the complaining type, and the two of them went off to the doctor. He examined my father and told him it was nothing more than indigestion. So my mother packed my father's lunch, or whatever it is you call the meal people eat who work all night (I have yet to come up with an appropriate label for the food I eat at Mutual at about 3 A.M.) and he went off to Kearny. He never came back. Before the end of his shift, as he was telling a joke to the guys in the plant, he keeled over, dead of a heart attack. He was 44 years old.

I'm grateful that I at least have memories of my father—as fragmented as they are. One thing was certain: both my parents doted on Lawrence Harvey Zeiger. I was particularly precious to them because they had lost a 6-year-old son to a burst appendix shortly before my birth on November 19, 1933. Because of that, any illness I had was magnified way out of proportion. One of my earliest memories is that of a mastoid operation at age 3. I had been bothered with frequent earaches as a very young child, but because one son had died on an emergency ward, my mother was loath to take me to the hospital.

Finally my ear was so bad that I absolutely had to have surgery. I remember my father telling me we were going to the circus. It's funny—even from 3 years old, I remember the double pain: the actual effects of the operation, and my father's lie. I remember the tubelike thing over my mouth, the smell of ether, the counting backward for Dr. Isadore Sackadorf, a giant of a man who made house calls until his death. I did end up forgiving my father his misrepresentation when recovery brought me a few toys and a lot of ice cream.

Because of my father's friendship with the local cops, I had a privileged relationship with them. My mother, who was an excellent seamstress, made me a miniature replica of a police uniform when I was 4 years old, and my father arranged for me to get a badge that read: LAWRENCE HARVEY ZEIGER, N.Y.C. POLICE. I also remember afternoons at the baseball stadium with my father. Maybe that has something to do with my passion for the game: an afternoon at the ball park is not just a throwback to some vague simpler, golden time; it is a throwback to a very specific time in my life.

When I turned 5½, it was time for Larry Zeiger to go to school. But I decided I was very happy with life as it was and declined to make the change. I think my mother might have been talked into keeping me home forever, but my father, as doting as he was, provided the discipline that my mother was never, even when she became the sole parent, able to provide. About two weeks into the school year, my father brought home with him one afternoon a very large man carrying a very large bag. The man told me he was the truant officer and that if I didn't decide on my own that I would go to school, he would have to put me into his bag and drag me there. I'm sure that the man was a friend of my father's and this was his idea of "psychology." In any case, it worked. I agreed to go to school on one condition: that I be made the eraser monitor. I wasn't exactly sure what the eraser monitor did, but I had heard some

of the older kids in the neighborhood talking about it and it
sounded terribly glamorous. In spite of all my protests, I found
I liked school—even when I wasn't cleaning the blackboards.
My second-grade teacher was Mrs. Egghouse (as Jack Paar
used to say, I kid you not). Mrs. Egghouse and I had a little
thing going. I won a writing contest in class for my composi-
tion "The Bumble Bees." I was madly in love with Mrs. Egghouse. I brought her apples. I'd try to finagle my way under the
desk so I could look at her legs. Even at age 6, I was a leg man,
and Mrs. Egghouse had great legs. I did so well in second
grade that I skipped right to fourth. Most of those years are a
blur, as they are for most people. One vivid incident stands
out. I was 8 years old and had broken my arm a few days earlier, so I was home from school, sitting by myself on the stoop.
Suddenly a huge black car pulled up and a suspicious-looking
man in a dark raincoat got out. "Hey, kid, come here. I've got
something for you," he said. My parents had told me repeatedly, Never, never talk to strangers. And particularly don't talk
to strangers who say they've got something for you. They were
so emphatic in their warnings that I got the impression there
were scores of dangerous strangers waiting to perform nefarious
acts on the youth of Brooklyn. I, of course, reassured my parents I would never talk to a stranger, particularly a stranger
who offered me something. It was an easy promise to keep because I'd never had an opportunity to break it—until that day
on the stoop. There I was facing my first moral dilemma. Do I
stay on the stoop and ignore the stranger? Or do I find out just
what he's got for me?

"What do you have?" I said to the man as I walked to the
car.

He opened the back door and showed me. It looked like
every comic book in the world, and I was a comic-book freak. It
turned out that my benefactor's son had disobeyed him; as a
punishment, this guy had taken his son's comic-book collec-

tion to give to the first kid he saw. I have to say this incident did nothing to enhance my faith in my parents' judgment: look what I got for disobeying them.

Broken arm and all, I carted my treasure up to the apartment. When my father came home from the store, he asked me where I'd gotten such riches. Very innocently I told him the story. He listened attentively until I got to the part about going over to the man's car. At which point he smacked me across the face so hard that I flew across the room. It was the only time he ever hit me; I'll never forget the back of his hand. My father did, however, let me keep the comic books. My father was a gentle man, but if he was crossed, he let you know about it. I can't fault my mother for the job she did raising us after my father died—she was strong, yet incredibly loving. But it was not in her nature to apply discipline; it was simply too painful for her. After my father died, I missed having a figure who could set some limits.

The rumors I had heard on the afternoon of his death came to pass: my brother and I were sent to camp—Camp Eden in Kingston, New York. The camp couldn't have been more ironically named. I had been living in Eden, and I had just been tossed out of it. I was as miserable there as I've ever been. I refused to talk to anyone, participate in any of the activities. I cried myself to sleep every night. Finally, in desperation, I walked into the neighboring town and sent my mother a wire. I don't know to this day how I knew about sending a wire, but I knew I had to do something to get out of there. My mother came up the next day and took us home. In all my confusion on the day of my father's death, I did see one thing clearly: I was right in knowing nothing would ever be the same again. That summer we moved from our third-floor walk-up to the Bensonhurst section of Brooklyn—to an attic apartment across the street from my mother's sister, my Aunt Bessie. When school started that fall, I had to begin all over again: new friends, new teachers, new surroundings. Larry, the whiz kid, never did well in school again; the things that had seemed important once just weren't important anymore.

My father had left practically no insurance—just enough to pay for his burial. So there we were, my mother with two little boys, and in those days there were no day-care centers. She didn't know what kind of job she could get—her working life had consisted of helping my father with the bar-and-grill; and she didn't want to leave us alone during the day even if she could find a job. We went on welfare, called relief in those days. Welfare is a debilitating mess. Anybody who tells me that people like being on welfare and enjoy its advantages doesn't know how demoralizing it is. I date my undying liberalism from that experience: if the City of New York hadn't been there to give us some sustenance, I don't know what we would have done.

Twice a month a welfare supervisor came, unannounced, to our attic to check things out. The inspector always wanted to know why there was meat in the refrigerator; he never believed that my mother bought it for her sons—she didn't have any. He wanted to know why we had a $3 shirt, instead of a $1 shirt. The inspectors did make sure our health was checked out. New York City bought me my first pair of glasses. Steel-rim jobs. Very in now, very out then.

One of the most ridiculous welfare rules is that people who are receiving assistance can't work. My mother was an accomplished seamstress and used to bring sewing into the house. If she was able to pick up $20 a week this way, it was a true godsend. But as soon as we'd hear the inspector's foot on the stairs, my brother, Marty, and I would run around madly hiding my mother's sewing. If she got caught, they cut off the checks. Wouldn't it make more sense to encourage people to work, to get some skills and independence which could lead to being free of welfare, instead of making work a crime? Finally she couldn't stand the indignity of it anymore, and when I turned 12 and Marty turned 8, my mother made arrangements with my Aunt Bessie to watch us after school when she went into "the city" (Manhattan was the city to us Brooklynites) for a job. Because of her sewing skill she went to work at a garment factory and eventually worked her way up to forewoman.

As I look back on it, I can only marvel at my mother's strength and endurance. She was 44 when my father died—which seemed impossibly old to me then, but of course, she was a relatively young woman. In spite of her age she never remarried; I don't think she was ever involved with a man again after my father's death. I remember a very few occasions when she did date. If there was any possibility of a romance, I think Marty and I did a fairly good job of killing it. Any man who showed up got the full treatment. We'd dress up in improvised capes and leap off furniture at him yelling, "Superman." We had dozens of tricks with matches, most of which entailed lighting them so close to the caller's face that his nasal hair was scorched.

No matter how bad I was, however, I was my mother's little angel. Whatever the trouble I got into as a child and as an adult, my mother would never believe anything bad about her Larry. If I were to blow up a bank and kill twenty-six people, my mother would have said, "Well, Larry made a mistake, but I'm sure those people at the bank did something to provoke him, so they are as much at fault as he is."

When I went to Florida and achieved some success, she was overflowing with pride. She came down and lived in Miami until her death in 1976, and her whole apartment was covered with photos of me and the people I had interviewed. When visitors came to her place, she would say, "Perhaps you know my son Larry. You don't? That's him in those pictures with some of his friends." When she went to the butcher store and she didn't like the way the lamb chops looked, she'd tell me she

said, "Don't you have better chops than this? No? Perhaps you
know my son Larry King." As soon as the butcher heard this,
she said, he'd take her in back and give her "the most beautiful
lamb chops."

Even though my mother did her best to raise us alone, I
used to take advantage of the fact that I was the boy without a
father. Whenever I got in trouble at school, I made sure the
teacher knew my father was dead. I used it to get comfort, attention, pity. Although fathers of friends were wonderful about
stepping in during fathers' days at school and things like that, I
remember being jealous of boys with fathers. In spite of the
rupture our move to Bensonhurst caused, I gradually came to
love the new neighborhood. Even though the Zeigers were
worse off than a lot of families in Bensonhurst, at best our
community was low-to-middle-class. In spite of our "depriva-
tion"—which we were not aware of—ours was a generation
that lived the American dream. I went to Layfayette High, and
the kids who graduated from there during my era are incredible: there are surgeons, judges, businessmen. Herb Cohen was
a classmate, as was Mutual president Marty Rubenstein.
Sandy Koufax graduated from the same school one year later.
Much of our success derived from the ideals instilled in us by
our parents, many of them immigrants who never achieved any
great success of their own. The most important thing in the
world to them was family. And the children of this tight, loving family structure were expected to be honest, hardworking
achievers. Although my own life has not been an exemplar of
carrying on this tradition, it's a great loss to society that so few
people are willing to make sacrifices, are willing to believe that
rewards need not be immediate, are willing to see a marriage
through even though it doesn't provide constant ecstasy.

In many ways the neighborhood was as important an influence on my own life as my immediate family. Bensonhurst
was like a small village—it was *Fiddler on the Roof* transposed

to America. The two major ethnic groups populating this corner of Brooklyn were Italians and Jews. These two groups share many characteristics: they are warm, family-oriented, hardworking and loud. On any afternoon near suppertime, windows started opening and you could hear a chorus of mothers yelling: "Tony!" "Vito!" "Myron!" "Seymour!" I was sure the whole world was Jewish and Italian, and I believed Italian was a religion as well as a country of origin. I suppose I knew from the movies that there were "regular" Americans—WASPs, as we now call them—but they lived in strange places with names like Ohio and Kansas.

What helped keep the neighborhood so self-contained was that it was unnecessary to leave it for any earthly need. There was the grocery store, Langer's, with its pickle barrel which we regularly dipped into. The bakery, Ebinger's, with its Charlotte russes; the movie theater; the candy store and the drugstore all were within walking distance, and it was axiomatic that if you wore your galoshes when it rained you would never have need for the drugstore; any malady from a cold to a broken leg was proof that the victim had neglected to put on his galoshes.

Of these establishments, the essential one was without doubt the candy store. The candy store was a place to get candy; it had jars of those wonderful 1-cent tooth-destroying sweets. But it was much more than that. It had a soda fountain—egg creams were considered the elixer of life—a few tables, newspapers and magazines, and a jukebox. For most of my childhood, the candy store was run by a man named Sam Maltz who had a hate-hate relationship with the kids in the neighborhood. He referred to us all as bandits, which he pronounced "ban-*deets.*" Since none of us ever had much money, Sam was always trying to throw us out of the store for loitering. "If you spend money, you can stay. Don't spend money, *out*" was his constant refrain. Once we felt Sam had said this just one time too many, so we took up a collection and got a couple of dollars' worth of change and went into the store.

"Sam, you said if we spend money we can stay," Herbie said.

"That's right. Spend money, you can stay," Sam replied.

"It doesn't matter what we spend it on?"

"No, just spend the money."

"We can spend it on anything?"

"*Anything. Just spend the money!*"

Sam had an explosive temper, and part of the fun of going to the candy store was provoking him into blowing up. Since he had given us the go-ahead, we went and spent money: we played Frankie Laine's recording of "Wild Goose" thirty-seven times on the jukebox. There's a line in it which says, "My heart goes where the wild goose goes," and the thirty-seventh time Frankie Laine sang that, Sam Maltz picked up the jukebox and tossed it onto the street, yelling, "You want to know where the wild goose goes? That's where the wild goose goes."

In spite of our periodic confrontations, Sam's candy store was where I first started reading newspapers. In those days New York had eight or ten newspapers, and Sam carried them all, including a couple of copies of the *Daily Worker* for any closet Communists in the neighborhood. I started reading the newspapers in order to get every possible interpretation of sports (even the *Daily Worker* had a sports page—presumably it covered sports from a collective point of view). Sam objected to my voracious reading for one reason: I never bought any of the newspapers. I tried to convince him that my reading them in the store didn't remove the ink from their pages, but we conducted a continuing battle on this issue.

Sports, particularly baseball, were and are an obsession with me. Several hours a day of my youth were devoted to reading about sports, seeing sporting events, arguing about the best players. Just as my neighborhood led me to believe that the world was made up of Jews and Italians, my boyhood interests led me to believe that for the most part the female of the species didn't exist. I knew there were girls. You'd see them at school; some of the guys even had sisters. But for the first sixteen or so years of my life, girls were mostly invisible.

Besides following professional sports, we had an active schedule of neighborhood sports. There were very few cars in Bensonhurst in those days, so most of our games were played on the street. There were the standards: baseball, touch football, stickball; as well as variations such as punchball, triangle ball and square ball. We also made up games. One we called nightball. This game was played, obviously, at night. We took turns standing under streetlamps, throwing a ball up above the arc of the lamplight and trying to catch it. It was harder to do than it sounds. Many of these games were played with a rubber ball we called a "spaldeen." It wasn't until years later that I realized the ball was actually a Spaulding pronounced with a Brooklyn accent. Although we needed no encouragement to hate the Japanese during the war, one result of the war with Japan really made us gung-ho: rubber was hard to get, so we were always low on "spaldeens."

Although my childhood has the nostalgic attraction of a more innocent time, I imagine it could have been terrible for the boys who weren't athletic, who were interested in academics or music. As far as we were concerned, they were sissies. To us accomplishment was measured in sewer covers: if you could hit a ball that traveled a certain number of sewer covers, you were golden.

Herbie Cohen once said that during the forties there were really three wars going on: there was World War II in which people we knew went off to fight and even die; there was the World War II we knew through the movies; and there were our own battles conducted with candy-counter ammunition in the movie theaters we frequented.

Compared with kids of today, we were, to say the least, unsophisticated, and our sources of information on the outside world were limited. For us, the movies provided the most powerful view of the world. Americans were like Gary Cooper, and Americans were brave, true, strong and good. Period. Every Saturday we went to the Benson Theater and had this knowledge reaffirmed. Because so many of the movies of that era were about the war, and because we wanted to emulate our heroes in whatever way we could, we conducted major battles right there in the Benson. In spite of the greatness of so many of the movies of the forties, Hollywood had a terrible habit of putting love scenes or musical numbers into these movies. Our sensibilities were righteously offended by this mush, and during these celluloid interludes we heaved our "ammo"—Jujubes and Goobers were favorites—at our enemies of the week. This ritualistic outburst caused small havoc among the adult customers, and the manager of the Benson wisely quarantined anyone under 18 in a sort of leper colony.

When we weren't at the movies, or in the candy store, or playing ball, we were on the stoop. The stoop was a social mecca—at least during our early years. When we became more mature, we graduated to the corner. On the stoop we sat and talked, made up games, argued about sports. Part of my skill as a broadcaster was honed on the stoop. During lulls in conversation—I've never been able to stand dead air—I announced passing cars or pedestrians. I also reconstructed, play by play, sporting events I'd gone to which the other guys might not have seen. I did the same thing with movies. It usually took me two hours and a half to tell the story of a ninety-minute film.

Even as a kid I was fascinated with radio, and wanted to be on it. I constantly fantasized about being an announcer—to be an announcer, I was sure, was to achieve the ultimate position in life. I wondered all about the announcers: were they as tall and distinguished as they sounded? did they stand or sit? where did they get breaking sports and news from? I used to walk down the street announcing to myself, oblivious as to how weird I must have looked. Some days I was Red Barber, the legendary voice of the Brooklyn Dodgers. Others I was Harry Von Zell, host of the *Eddie Cantor Show*. Still others, I was Ed Herlihy, the announcer on the old *Children's Hour* on Sunday mornings. When I think back on it, the phrases I practiced over and over again come back instantly: "It's cloudy in Chicago today as the Dodgers start a six-game road trip." "The *Gillette Cavalcade of Sports* is on the air." "This is the Columbia Broadcasting System." "And now, *The Romance of Helen Trent*." "Jell-o presents *The Jack Benny Show*." I practiced all this in front of a mirror holding a rolled-up newspaper. Whenever I was out sick from school I'd listen to all the soaps and bring everyone up to date on what was happening, and believe me, my versions were no mere synopses.

When I first moved to Bensonhurst, before I got to know anybody, the radio was my only friend. It was the first thing I saw in the morning, and the last thing I heard at night. Part of its impact came from its sheer physical presence. It was large, of polished dark wood and shaped like a temple. In his book *Working*, Studs Terkel points out that very few people end up doing what they would like to do for their livelihood. I am one of the lucky ones in that respect. I got to go inside the temple.

As much as I fantasized about being on the radio, I had absolutely no idea how I would get from my Brooklyn bedroom to a radio studio: which must make me sound like a total dimwit to kids of today who are interested in broadcasting and take courses in it in junior high school. Sometimes, however, I worry about the single-mindedness of the kids I see who want to be on radio or television, who have majored in broadcasting in college and have spent every summer getting internships in the field. They are missing something if they never take advantage of their time in school to learn something about history, literature or science, and if they never spend any time in the world outside a studio. The listeners also lose when their sources of information know little of life beyond microphone range.

But back when I was a teen-ager in Brooklyn, the last thing I worried about was how to fulfill my fantasies of becoming a broadcaster. My number one concern was having a good time. Now, having a good time often involved an element of getting into trouble. This presented many crises of conscience, because I also felt a need to live up to the expectations the world placed on any nice Jewish boy. So I was constantly having to weigh the ratio of fun to trouble and decide accordingly. Often, however, this rational process got short-circuited when I found myself going along with anything Herbie Cohen proposed. Today Herb is a best-selling author, a zillionaire consultant on negotiating and an all-around upstanding member of the community. Back in Brooklyn, Herbie was, as they say in Yiddish, a trombenik. And Larry Zeiger was always willing to go along for the ride.

Not all Herb's enterprises were nefarious. There was the time when his inspiration made us at age 13 the hits of the Bensonhurst theater circuit. Our triumph came about, as usual, because we originally intended to provoke trouble.

Our eighth-grade class was putting on its yearly show for the parents and the rest of the school. The theme was a Gay Nineties revue, with songs such as "By the Sea" and "The Band Played On." Herbie and I were given parts of about thirty seconds in duration each because we were rightly perceived as troublemakers who couldn't be trusted for more than half a minute at a time. The star of the show was our classmate Sol Schwartz, a.k.a. Sol the Worrier. Today one of those counselors for troubled youths the school systems have would have recognized that Sol truly had a problem which could have used professional help. But to us Sol was simply someone who provided endless opportunities for harassment. For example, in math class the teacher wrote on the blackboard that our homework that night was problems 1, 3, 7, 8 and 12. After everyone copied down the assignment, she erased it. Immediately after she erased it, Sol raised his hand and said, "Mrs. Parker I just wanted to double-check the homework tonight. It's problems 1, 3, 7, 8 and 12." "That's right, Sol," Mrs. Parker said. "Problems 1, 3, 7, 8 and 12?" "Yes, Sol, you have it correct." Class would let out, but before Sol left he'd turn to me and say, "Larry, the homework is 1, 3, 7, 8 and 12. Right?" "Gee, Sol, I have 1, 3, 5, 6 and 11." "You have 1, 3, 5, 6 and 11?" "That's right—I copied it off the board," I said.

Sol was now in a panic, and he went up to the teacher and got a confirmation of the original assignment. Then we'd tell Herbie or someone else who had had Mrs. Parker earlier in the day to go up to Sol and say, "Sol, I just want to double-check the homework with you. It's problems 2, 4, 5, 9 and 13. Right?" Sol would be sweating by this time when he repeated the assignment he had written down. "That's funny. You wouldn't think she'd give us all different assignments," Herbie said. "I don't know what to do," Sol said. "If I were you, Sol, I'd do them all. You don't want to end up doing the wrong assignment; that would be very bad," Herbie said. That night Sol would call both Herbie and me to double-check the assignment, and of course we each gave him a totally different assignment. Sol usually ended the night by calling the teacher at home to get a final word from her. He was the only kid we ever knew who called a teacher.

In spite of his insecurity problem, Sol was a very talented singer, and in the Gay Nineties production he was the master of ceremonies and also in most of the musical numbers. As the day of the performance approached, Sol became nearly catatonic with anxiety. Finally, Sunday night, the evening before the premiere, Sol came out looking for his good friends Herbie and me to have us allay his fears. When he found us on Herbie's stoop, Sol looked like a candidate for a straitjacket.

"I can't do it," he said; "it's too much for me."

"Sol, stop worrying. Now, what's the worst thing that could happen?" I said. "The worst thing that could happen is that you totally screw up and you make a fool of yourself in front of your family and all your friends."

"Sol, I have to agree with you," Herbie added. "I saw the rehearsal, and I think you have good reason to worry."

A few minutes into this conversation and Sol was ready for a rest home. Finally he said to us, "Listen, guys, you have to rescue me. I can't do it. You've got to go on for me."

This was the night before the show, and the two of us knew only our own thirty seconds' worth of dialogue. But since we were tremendous hams, we figured we'd do it. The two of us invented a couple of vaudeville-type characters called Spark and Plug (Funny, huh?) and worked out a few routines. We decided we'd have to improvise the rest of the material in between the musical numbers which had been already worked out.

Opening night came, Sol was safely in the audience and the two of us were behind the curtain. The curtain rose and Herbie said to me, "Hi, Spark." I said to Herbie, "Hi, Plug," and we were off.

"I know a joke about a chicken," Herbie said.

"Oh, yes?" I replied.

"But I don't think I'll pullet," he said.

"I'd duck it if I were you."

"Oh, that was fowl."

"You know what I do for a living?" I said.

"No, what?" Herbie replied.

"I'm a mechanic at Madison Square Garden."

"What does that involve?"

"I fix fights."

Now, this was really bad stuff. Corny, bad stuff. Herbie and

I knew it was terrible, but for some reason the audience loved it. They couldn't get enough. We had to do an encore. The show was such a hit that we toured it to other schools and community groups. Maybe the success lay partly in the fact that it showed through that these two 13-year-olds knew this stuff was cornball. Instead of being jealous, Sol the Worrier was enormously grateful to us. In spite of his paralyzing stage fright, Sol Americanized his name and ended up becoming a professional entertainer. He probably could have had a much more successful career than he had, but his mobility was limited by his constant fear of bad weather, dangerous electrical wiring and audiences.

Most of our capers did not turn out as felicitously as Spark and Plug. One of our most notorious was the Mel Moppo incident. Herbie and I were by this time ninth-graders at Junior High School 128 in Brooklyn. Our class was divided into four sections: 9B-1, 9B-2, 9B-3 and 9B-4. Herbie and I were in class 9B-4, also known as the class for incorrigibles. In 9B-4, Herbie and I hung around most often with two other kids, Brazzy Abate, who became a neurosurgeon, and Melvin Goldfarb, whom we called Mel Moppo because he had a head of wild, curly hair which looked like a mop to us. The four of us were constant companions, and when Mel was absent from school for several days in a row, we three became concerned and decided to investigate. So off we trooped to Mel Moppo's house.

When we got to Mel Moppo's house, Mel Moppo's cousin was sitting on the stoop looking lonely and sad, and all the shades were drawn. It was a heart-rending sight. Herbie looked at this and said, "Hey, why are you sitting here looking all forlorn?" And Mel Moppo's cousin said, "Melvin has developed a case of tuberculosis, and Melvin's parent's have taken him to Phoenix for the cure. I'm supposed to close up the house and notify the school that Melvin won't be able to finish the semester and to have his records transferred to Lafayette High School."

Now, this was March or April of our last semester in junior high, so the school system was obviously going to graduate Mel Moppo, since he was going to miss only a few months of school.

Herbie then said to Mel Moppo's cousin, "Listen, you have enough to worry about without having to do down to the school to give them this unhappy news. You just pack up and go to Phoenix and we young men will notify the authorities of Melvin's illness."

Even though Mel Moppo was our friend, I had the suspicion that Herbie was not making this offer out of the goodness of his heart; but I couldn't imagine why he was making it. Anyway, Brazzy and I chimed in that we would certainly make sure the junior high was notified about Melvin. So Mel Moppo's cousin thanked us and finished packing and left for Phoenix.

Herbie, Brazzy and I walked back to our corner, two of us waiting for Herbie's explanation. I must digress here for a moment to explain about Brooklyn street corners. Ours was Eighty-sixth Street and Bay Parkway, and believe me, it was *our* corner. You've seen those *National Geographic* films about moose staking out their territory and woe be unto another moose who makes a play for some already claimed piece of forest; well, that's what street corners were like in Brooklyn. So we walked back to our corner and Herbie said, "I have an idea that could make us five dollars apiece to spend at Nathan's." Nathan's was a very popular hot dog place about six minutes from our corner.

"Tomorrow we will go to Mrs. Dewar and tell her Mel Moppo died," Herbie explained. "The school, of course, will call his house: no answer, because the phone's been disconnected. Moppo is in Phoenix, and no one but us knows he's in Phoenix. We raise money in class for flowers. We take the money and go to Nathan's. If we get fifty cents a kid and there are thirty kids in class, that's fifteen dollars—five dollars apiece. It can't fail."

When I told Herbie of my one reservation, that Mel Moppo was not dead and would show up at Lafayette High in the fall, Herbie had an irrefutable argument: by the time fall rolls around everyone will forget Mel Moppo was supposed to be dead, and fifteen bucks is fifteen bucks. It was very convincing at the time.

The next day Herbie, Brazzy and I went to our homeroom teacher, Mrs. Dewar. We had our heads down, tears in our eyes: we convincingly looked as if our best friend had just died. We told her about Mel Moppo. Now, Moppo had been a sickly boy, so the news wasn't that incredible. Maintaining her cool so as not to alarm the rest of the class, Mrs. Dewar walked us to the office to report the news. A secretary there, who must have known our reputation, wasn't just going to take our word for it. She called Mel Moppo's house, and got a message saying the line had been disconnected. So she pulled out Mel Moppo's card and wrote *"Deceased"* across it. Deceased! They believed us!

We went back to class and told Mrs. Dewar we wanted to collect money for a fund to send flowers to Mel Moppo's funeral. Just as Herbie had predicted, everyone donated 50 cents; and the three of us went down to Nathan's and gorged ourselves and had a ball. We figured that was the end of the story.

Two weeks later, Mrs. Dewar called us up to the front of the class and told us we were wanted in the principal's office. Now, this sent us into a bit of a panic. We were sure they had found out. On our way down the corridor, as Brazzy and I saw our futures, such as they were, go down the toilet, Herbie kept saying, "Don't worry, don't worry. We'll say we heard he died, we sent the flowers to charity and we'll promise to give the money back. Don't worry, don't worry."

When we got to the office, we expected a hysterical scene. Instead, the principal, Dr. Ira Levy, was there smiling.

"Welcome, young lads," he said. "Welcome, Herbert, Lawrence, Brazzy. Please sit down."

Brazzy and I were ready to confess, and Herbie was giving us the "Don't say anything" signal.

"Young gentlemen, I have some important news for you. The junior high school administrators of New York City have gotten together and decided that junior high schools don't have the same individual image or school spirit that our high schools have, and we would like to correct this situation. Each junior high school in the City of New York is going to have a project, and *The New York Times* is going to do a series of stories on these projects.

"We had a faculty meeting today and decided that what you three wonderful young men did for your late friend Melvin Goldfarb would make a fine project.

"At Junior High School 128, we are going to start a Melvin Goldfarb Memorial Award. We will honor each year's outstanding senior with this award in memory of your friend."

As I reflect on this incident, it becomes clear to me that there and then was the moment to say, "Doc, we have a little something to tell you." But we got carried away with the ego and the emotion of the moment; for the first time in our lives we were in favor with the head man. I even tried to convince myself that Mel Moppo really was dead.

Back to class we went, where we were assigned to be the student representatives for the Melvin Goldfarb Memorial Award. Two weeks before graduation it was decided to have a ceremony honoring the first recipient of the award. Finally the morning of the ceremony rolled around.

The entire school assembled in the auditorium for this solemn occasion. On stage was a huge banner which read, "MELVIN GOLDFARB MEMORIAL FUND." Below that was displayed the Melvin Goldfarb Memorial Plaque. Dr. Levy was on stage behind the lectern. Next to him, in our best suits, were Herbie, Brazzy, and Larry. In the front row was a guy from *The New York Times* and his photographer.

And on that day, that very day, Mel Moppo came back to

school. He had made what they called in Phoenix the most dramatic recovery in the history of tubercular treatment. Yes, Mel Moppo came back to school that day, but he came back a little late. When Moppo arrived at school, everyone was at the assembly. When Moppo went to class and found no one there, he went down to the office to find out what was going on. They had no idea who he was in the office, so they told him to hurry up and go to the auditorium.

Moppo went to the auditorium and slowly began opening the doors in order to sneak in late. The doors to the auditorium were two big, squeaky brass jobs, and Moppo was slowly opening the door, and the first thing he saw was his name on a banner. The second thing he saw was the word "MEMORIAL." Mel Moppo may not have had too much going on under the mop, but he was not so dumb that he didn't know what "memorial" meant next to his name. Now, New York kids are hip, and as the kids in the back row spotted Mel Moppo they immediately realized what had happened: Herbie, Brazzy and Larry had put one over on them for 50 cents a pop. The laughter started to move through the auditorium as more and more kids realized what had happened. Dr. Levy, who did not know Moppo from a funeral wreath, put on his glasses and was trying to figure out what was going on. Moppo looked at the stage in a total panic, which nearly matched the expressions of Brazzy and me. Herbie, as usual, looked cool. By now half the audience was laughing, Dr. Levy was asking who was that kid and the rest of the place was in total confusion. Suddenly Herbie stood up, went to the front of the stage and yelled, "Moppo, go home. You're dead!"

Moppo tore through the doors and ran home, his hair straightening along the way. After that, the place was total pandemonium. *The New York Times* guys were on the floor. And Dr. Levy was—well, Dr. Levy was clearly displeased. He looked at the three of us and told us to go to the office immediately, and he stormed off the stage. Brazzy was practically in tears; he kept moaning something like "I could have been a brain surgeon, I could have been a brain surgeon." I figured this incident would leave me an orphan because my mother would die when she heard about it. And Herbie, as usual, was saying, "Don't worry, don't worry, we'll handle it, don't worry."

The New York Times reporter followed us to the office with tears rolling down his face, he thought it was so funny. We got into Dr. Levy's office. He looked at us and said—this isn't an exact quote, but it captures the essence of what he said: "You three are suspended from school for life. It is also recommended that you be sent to Rikers Island, where you will be put at hard labor until you are eighteen, at which time we have no further control over you, to our regret. You three have pulled the most dastardly act I have ever seen. You three have criminal minds—"

Herbie interrupted this tirade by saying, "Wait a minute, Dr. Levy: you are making a big mistake."

Brazzy and I looked at Herbie wondering what he was going to try to pull.

"What did you say?" replied Dr. Levy.

"Dr. Levy, let's talk this out," Herbie continued. "We did a bad thing—the three of us are happy to admit that. But if you suspend us, there will automatically be a hearing before the Board of Education. At that hearing they are definitely going to agree that we deserve to be suspended for life. But they are also going to have a question for you. They are going to want to know why you took the word of three nincompoops that a kid is dead, and for confirmation all you got was a message by the phone company that the line was disconnected. We may be suspended, but you're out of work."

After Herbie's speech Dr. Levy just sat there, a shell of his former self. The man was whipped, totally whipped. The man from the *Times,* who had been listening to this in the outer office, came in to say that he wasn't going to print the story because no one would ever believe it. There we were. The *Times* guy agreed not to print the story; Dr. Levy agreed not to suspend us; we agreed to return the $15. By the way, to this day, thirty-five years later, Mel Moppo, who owns a furniture-moving business in Phoenix, does not understand the whole thing. We tried several times to explain it to him: "It's okay, Moppo—we took the money and went to Nathan's; you weren't dead." He never got it.

Two weeks later graduation day rolled around. On graduation day, section 9B-4 was lined up to graduate. Dr. Levy was on stage again, this time handing out diplomas. Our section was fairly small, so Moppo was only a few people behind Herbie. Herbie got his diploma, and Moppo moved forward. As Moppo went to take his diploma, Herbie rushed back to the podium, moved Moppo aside and said, "I'll take it, Dr. Levy; he's dead."

ALTHOUGH I CAN'T EXCUSE our behavior as adolescents, sometimes I felt all the trouble we got into wasn't quite our fault. Sometimes it just seemed like fate. For example, one evening when Herbie and I were about 15, we went out on a double date. This was a historic event in our lives, since we were rather retarded as far as the opposite sex was concerned. But the date had been a big success; I think we took the girls to Sam Maltz's for egg creams, or something equally exciting. After we walked the girls home, Herbie and I went to our regular corner to discuss our triumph. As we were standing there a police car pulled up to us and one of the cops inside said, "Okay, you two, get in." I protested that something was wrong: we had just dropped our dates off and were innocently standing on the corner. Herbie, by this time in the back seat, looked at me, looked at the cop and said, "Larry, when they got us, they got us."

What had happened was that two other boys who fitted our description had been vandalizing the neighborhood and the cops figured we were the suspects. On the way to the police station I was crying, telling the policemen that they were making a big mistake, and Herbie was saying stuff like "Larry, I told you justice would catch up with us." At the precinct house they put us in separate rooms for questioning. Since I had had nothing to do with the vandalism, I simply sat there and bawled, "I'm innocent, I'm innocent." I later found out that during his interrogation Herbie was confessing to every crime on the books; I think he even claimed responsibility for Pearl Harbor. Finally, some genius figured out that these two goofballs probably wouldn't be able to figure out how to vandalize each other's shoelaces, and called our parents to pick us up. It wasn't every day that Bensonhurst parents got calls from the police station about their sons, and naturally our parents alerted practically the whole neighborhood. Coming down to the station to get us, in addition to my mother and Herbie's parents, were siblings, aunts, uncles and friends. When they brought us out, Herbie looked at the crowd and yelled, "They got the whole gang!"

To say the least, the cops were not amused. As punishment for wasting so much of their time they pulled Herbie's Police Athletic League pass, which allowed free attendance at Yankee games.

ONE OF THE MOST important aspects of my life from ages 14 through 19 was belonging to the Warriors. We called it a gang—a word that has implications today it didn't have back

in the forties and early fifties. The Warriors were really an
S.A.C.—a social/athletic club—and we met every Sunday in
Warrior Bernie Horowitz's basement. The club gave me a
sense of belonging and a source of male camaraderie that is
particularly important to a fatherless boy.

Naturally the Warriors had a jacket. No self-respecting club
was without a jacket. Ours was a beauty; I wish I still had it. It
was red with a white stripe along the sleeves, wool on the outside, satin on the inside. On the back was an Indian head, on
the left front was my name in script and on the right front my
number. As the Warriors got further along in their teens, a
disturbing phenomenon began to occur: Warrior girlfriends
were seen sporting the sacred Warrior jacket. It was sort of like
being pinned. Finally the problem got so bad we had a club
meeting to discuss it. There was some lobbying for the passage
of a rule forbidding females to wear the jacket. This faction
was led, naturally, by guys who couldn't get girlfriends, which
included me and Herbie. Finally it was decided members
would stop the practice voluntarily, without the passage of a
law.

While we took S.A.C. athletics very seriously—Brooklyn
clubs had a regular schedule of league matches—the social
aspect of the club was by no means eclipsed by sports. The
character of the club was very much influenced by its
location in the Horowitzes' basement. The Horowitzes were
truly an extended family. There was Bernie and his older
brother, Leon; their parents, Nathan and Dora; Dora's sister
and brother-in-law; and Dora's mother, Bubba. Every one of
them was a character, and we all got caught up in the family
saga.

Bernie's father was a furrier, and the family was fairly well-
to-do for the neighborhood, which meant it was middle-class.
Bubba, since coming to America from Russia, had also managed to acquire some money—how, we never knew—which

she was closely guarding for her old age. The only problem was
that Bubba appeared to be immortal. As she approached 100,
her health was not good, but she nonetheless defied all medical
predictions of her demise. She regularly outlived her doctors.
One poor man, about 40, came over to examine Bubba and
told Dora, "Your mother won't live out the week." The doctor
went home and died of a heart attack, and Bubba kept going
and going. One of Bubba's many problems was poor circula-
tion. To help remedy this, her family rolled her around on the
living-room floor to keep her blood moving. A regular feature
of the Warriors meeting was listening to Bubba being rolled
around above us.

Finally, the unthinkable happened: Bubba died. We had all
come to like Bubba and were saddened by her passing, but
what made it particularly painful was that she died three days
before New Year's, for which we had planned a huge party.
Bubba's demise threw quite a wrench into our plans. Naturally, the Horowitzes asked that the party be called off; after
all, they were sitting shiva for Bubba. While we were sorry
about Bubba's death, we didn't think it necessitated the can-
cellation of our party; so we sent Herbie to negotiate with the
Horowitzes. At first he took a tough-guy approach. He said to
Dora, "Bubba did this on purpose. She never liked it when we
had parties, and she did this to spite us."

This tack was noticeably unsuccessful with Mrs. Horowitz,
so ever-resourceful Herbie tried another approach.

"Mrs. Horowitz, you know Bubba would have wanted the
party to go on," he said. "She would want us to have some joy
as we remembered her."

We couldn't believe it. The Horowitzes gave in and allowed
us to have the party. I should have known then that Herbie's
future success as a negotiator was assured. We did make a con-
cession to Bubba's death, however. We hung only black crepe
paper in the clubroom, and at midnight instead of loudly wel-

coming in the New Year, we observed a moment of silence for Bubba.

Most of our contact with the Horowitz family was through fellow Warrior Bernie. Bernie was one of the most generous, kindhearted guys I've ever known. He was also one of the funniest, although Bernie was not always aware how funny he was. Bernie was in no danger of receiving a Rhodes Scholarship, but he didn't want anyone else to catch on to this, so he developed one of the most unusual speech patterns I've ever heard. He sounded like a cross between the Crazy Guggenham character on the old *Jackie Gleason Show*—you know: that sort of "deze and doze" voice—and a proper British gentleman.

The Warriors were all sports fanatics, and we were all perpetually broke, which made attending all the events we wanted to see a little difficult. We didn't let it thwart us completely, however. For example, we used to go to Madison Square Garden in the afternoon and watch minor-league hockey, then retire to the men's room and remain there until the New York Rangers took to the ice in the evening. The management was wise to kids' hiding in the restroom between games and had someone check it out. What he didn't do, though, was check the stalls. In each of the six stalls was a Warrior with his feet up on the door reading the newspaper. We'd sit there for two hours, feet up, reading the paper, then go out and see the Rangers.

We also used to sneak from the upper deck to the lower deck at Ebbets Field, where the Brooklyn Dodgers played. Once when a bunch of us were sneaking through the fence that separated the two, Bernie got stuck. There he was, half of him in the upper deck, half in the lower. The rest of us had gotten through, and we were rolling in the stands, helpless with laughter. While Bernie was trying to extricate himself, a cop came along and asked Bernie what the hell he was doing. Bernie very casually started reading through his program as if this were the most natural position in the world to be in. He then looked up at the policeman and said in the unique voice, "Pardon me, Officer, sir, but this is my preferred method of observing the sporting event."

Nicknames were very important to the Warriors, and they usually sprang from observation of the personality, such as Sol the Worrier, or looks, such as Mel Moppo. Herbie's was Handsomo—because he suffered under the delusion he was good-looking. Mine was Zeke—a variation on Zeiger. Bernie's nickname was Who-Ha—one of the few to be invented by their bearers. One day we were sitting around in the clubroom talking about sports when someone called out to Bernie, "Hey, Bernie," to which Bernie replied, "Who?" "What do you mean, 'Who'? I'm asking you something." "Ha?" Bernie responded. Thus a nickname was born: Who-Ha.

Even as a teen-ager I was chronically in need of funds, and Who-Ha took the role of my main benefactor. The nice thing about Who-Ha was that I never had to ask him for money; he always knew I needed it. "Larry, I would like to give you a few dollars because these are excess funds for me, and I would like to see them benefiting my good friend." So I'd borrow a couple of bucks from Who-Ha. What invariably happened was that I'd get into a heated discussion with him over baseball teams, or something like that. Now, Who-Ha's debating skills were not quite up to those of William Buckley. Pretty quickly the discussion would degenerate into Who-Ha's saying, "If you're so smart, I would like back the ten dollars you owe me that you never repaid."

"Bernie, I don't have the ten dollars right now," I'd reply.

"I said give me the money you owe me!" he'd say.

Usually one of us ended up stomping out, which was a pretty effective way of ending the discussion. Eventually I'd get together the money I owed Bernie and go give it to him.

"Bernie, here's the ten bucks I owe you."

"What do I want ten bucks for?" he'd say.

"You told me last week that I was a welsher and that you wanted your money back."

"Larry, you're my friend. Keep the money. You need it more than I do."

Of course Bernie never wanted the money back. It was the only form of leverage he had for getting out of losing debates.

AT ONE POINT the Warriors merged with a smaller local club. It was a great deal: not only did we get to keep the Warrior name, we acquired Sandy Koufax, who at that time was one of the city's top high school basketball players. We knew Sandy was a great athlete, but when we thought of him we thought of basketball, not baseball. Of all the Warriors, Sandy was the best example of a nice Jewish boy. He was quiet, respectful, hardworking, a wonderful son. In spite of this we all liked Sandy. When he first signed with the Dodgers, I remember how thrilled we all were. They gave him number 32, which he hated; he had always worn number 8 in high school. It's funny, but 32 has become a famous sports number. Sandy wore it; in football, O. J. Simpson and Jim Brown wore it. The first season Sandy played with the Dodgers, a group of us tried to go to every game. While he was in a dugout we would move down the stands and lean over near the dugout and yell, "Hey, Sandy, we brought your matzoh sandwiches." Matzoh sandwiches are a Jewish delicacy of matzoh, which is unleavened bread with the look and consistency of cardboard, and chicken fat, which is called shmaltz.

As we leaned over and tried to hand these to Sandy, he would wave us away while pretending not to see us. Jackie Robinson and all the famous Dodgers were in the dugout and there we were, trying to get matzoh sandwiches to Sandy. He was not too thrilled. Finally the manager, Walt Alston, asked what the hell a matzoh sandwich was, and we ended up passing these things around to the team. It was quite a sight to see all the dodgers except Sandy eating matzoh sandwiches.

AS I'VE SAID, as we got along in our teens our obsession with sports was somewhat eclipsed by an interest in girls. Whenever any Warrior had a date, the following night at the club he was greeted with a barrage of "D'ya get it?" Now, we had no idea what "it" was. If I had been getting "it" I wouldn't have known what to do with "it." There were a few approved responses to this question. One was to say, yes, indeed you had gotten "it." The other was to reply with some sort of aphorism. One popular one was "The anticipation is greater than the reality." We didn't know what that meant either, but it seemed to answer the question about "it."

As we got to be about 16, most of the Warriors managed to have girlfriends at one time or another. All except Herbie and me, who apparently were experiencing an extremely delayed puberty. We found ourselves increasingly frustrated in our attempts to get together a group of guys to go to a basketball game or hockey game on the weekends. They were all spending Saturday evening with Shirley or Vivien. Because Herbie and I spent every weekend with each other, we started to get a considerable amount of abuse. Finally we had had enough and decided it was time to fight back. The two of us went to the local Woolworth's and purchased a wallet. A feature of any cheapo wallet is that it has pictures of models or starlets inside it. That weekend, when the guys started razzing us about spending it together, Herbie said, "Well, we're going to have some company." This got all of the club members very much interested. "Yeah, who's the company?" they wanted to know.

"We're going to see Miriam," Herbie said.

"Who's Miriam?" Bernie said. "I don't know any Miriam."

"She's a friend of ours," I said.

"Come on, there's no Miriam," said a Warrior nicknamed Gutter Rat.

"Yes, there is; we met her last week," I said.

"Prove it," Gutter Rat said.

With that, Herbie pulled out the wallet and showed everyone the picture of the beautiful model that had come with it. On it we had inscribed: *"To Herbie and Larry. My two favorite men. Love, Miriam."*

"Jeez, she's beautiful!" Bernie said. "What's her last name?"

"Glick. Her name is Miriam Glick," I said.

That was it. Those guys were so dumb that they bought it. For more than a year Herbie and I spent just about every weekend with our beloved Miriam. All the other guys were jealous, because Miriam was the most agreeable person ever to walk the face of the earth. When other guys' girlfriends wanted to be taken to Manhattan for Saturday night, Miriam wanted to go see a Knicks game with us. Anything we wanted to do, Miriam went along. Herbie and I hated to have to give her up for real girls.

In spite of our social retardation, Herbie and I did manage to get a very occasional date during the time we were simultaneously going out with Miriam. On one occasion, the two of us actually managed to lure two girls back to the clubhouse, which was used as a lovers' hideaway on various nights of the week by different Warriors. On this night, there was no one else there, so we ushered the two girls in. Then I used a failproof Warrior seduction line on them: "Want to see our 'W' light up?"

On the floor of Bernie's basement the Warriors had painted a "W" in luminous paint. In order to see it light up, one naturally had to shut off the lights—oh, were we clever!

"Sure," said one of the girls.

Off went the light, onto the girls we dived and miracle of miracles, they didn't throw us off. We weren't getting "it," but we were getting something. After a few minutes of making out, one of the girls said, "Don't you have a radio? I like it better when there's a radio."

I like it better when there's a radio! Had we hit the jackpot! The only problem was that the Warrior radio was on the blink. This was desperation time, but I was not about to let this opportunity slip away. I knew Bernie had a radio in his bedroom, so I told the girls to just be patient while I slipped upstairs and borrowed the radio.

When I got upstairs I was greeted by Bernie's mother, Dora, sitting like a sentry near the basement door, a huge wooden bowl in her lap in which she was chopping liver.

"Hi, Dora," I said. "I just came to borrow Bernie's radio."

"What do you want with a radio?"

"Oh, Herbie and I just wanted to catch the game."

"You got girls down there, that's why you want a radio, isn't it?"

"Dora, really, Herbie and I just want to listen to the game. There are no girls."

"Don't lie to me. I have a sixth sense. There are girls down there, and you're not getting any radio!"

"Dora, Bernie told me I could borrow his radio and I'm just going to get his radio."

"You're not going anywhere."

"Dora, I told you, I need the radio, and I'm going to get the radio."

With that, Dora stood up, holding the wooden bowl like a shield, and blocked my way down the hall to Bernie's bedroom.

"Listen Dora, don't be unreasonable: I just want the radio."

"Radio, shmadio, you're not getting any radio."

"Dora, I'm warning you . . ."

What happened next is a little unclear. I certainly never intended to harm Dora; I just wanted to get at that radio. As I started down the hall, she put out an arm to block me, which I pushed away, causing Dora to fall backward, covering herself with chopped liver. I kept going, got the radio and went downstairs.

Our exchange had been so loud that Herbie had come to the top of the stairs to see what was going on. When I got back down to the clubroom, Herbie said, "Hey, Larry, I don't think Bernie's going to be too pleased when he finds out you knocked over his mother."

"I didn't knock her over; she just wouldn't get out of my way," I said.

Anyway, I plugged in the radio and prepared to return to activities. After about thirty seconds of which, both girls decided it was time to go home.

The next day Bernie came looking for me, and he was mad. "Hey, Larry, what's the idea of hitting my mother?" he said.

"I didn't hit your mother; she assaulted me and I was just defending myself."

"Yeah, you beat up my mother, and she got chopped-liver stains all over her dress, and we couldn't eat the chopped liver for dinner, and my father got very upset."

"Did you tell me I could use your radio? I just went to use your radio."

"Yeah, but I didn't tell you you could beat up my mother to get it. Here's what I'm going to do if you ever touch my mother again. I'm going to find *your* mother and sock her in the face."

"You sock my mother in the face and I'm going to break both your mother's arms," I said.

"Yeah. You break both my mother's arms and I'll break your mother's arms and legs."

Macho guys that we were, we both carefully avoided any reference to hitting each other—you could get hurt that way.

Word of the fight spread quickly, and everyone thought Bernie and I would have a real feud, but since neither of us had any desire to tangle with the other's mother either, we made up after a couple of days.

As much as I would have liked it to be the case, not all of my teen-age years were spent with the Warriors. There was that small—and for me it was a small—intrusion called school. Every so often a teacher or subject would catch my imagination, and I would do quite well in something. For the most part, though, after my father died I more or less sleepwalked through school. This was in direct contrast to my brother, Martin, who was a good and conscientious student who got scholarships to both college and law school. He is now a vice president and corporate counsel for the Revco drugstore chain. My mother never bugged me to do better in school or be more like Marty: I was her pride and joy; she wasn't capable of finding fault.

At this point I really should digress a little about my relationship with Marty. The two of us are closer now than we've ever been in our lives—which, after all, isn't really unusual. Many siblings finally get to be friends after they become adults and can really enjoy each other without rivalry.

Marty and I were never close as kids—for a variety of reasons, I think. There was just enough of an age difference between us that we were always at two different stages of development, so to me he was more a kid brother than a playmate. Also, the specter of the brother who had died had faded by the time Marty came along, so Marty never got the obsessive attention from my mother that I did. Naturally, he resented that, and whatever sibling rivalry normally exists between two boys was sharpened because of it. For example, Marty was always conscientious, got good grades in school—yet goof-off that I was, I got all the attention.

During the time of my problems, after I was out of work, Marty and I had no relationship at all. Marty is disciplined, hardworking, conservative. He probably has the first dollar he ever made. I have a lot of respect for him—respect that he could not reciprocate for a long time. He was, and rightly so, disgusted with what I had done with my life and wanted nothing to do with me. I made no attempt to explain myself to him; I had no explanation to give.

Since I have been doing the show on Mutual, Marty and I have become friends. It's not because I have become well known. It's because I have become, I hope, a brother who is worthy of his respect.

Marty comes to Washington from Cleveland quite often on business, so we are seeing each other more than we have since we were boys. And his two children, Scott, a senior at the University of Florida, and Elise, a senior in high school, have both stayed with me during the summer. We have become a family again.

If my mother was not capable of finding fault, there were those in the school system who were. I was the kind of kid who was a borderline troublemaker. Troublemaker does not have the same connotation today—today a troublemaker is a kid who stabs teachers or sells dope in the hall. In my day it was the kind of kid who organized humming. You know—the teacher would be at the blackboard and all of a sudden the room would sound like an invasion of locusts. The genius of group humming was that you could never tell who organized it, or who was doing it and who wasn't.

Although I was a bad student, I don't think the fault was completely mine. There was an underlying attitude in the school system that we were barbarians, or at least the offspring of barbarians, and that they were going to civilize us.

For example, we had a Music Appreciation course. Instead of having us listen to symphonies and discussing the composers and the history of music, they had us memorize the tunes of

famous compositions. How did they do that? By making up
awful little rhymes that we had to sing along to them. For example, to memorize Percy Grainger's "Country Gardens," we
had to sing endlessly: " 'Coun-tree-ee Gar-dens,' 'Coun-tree-ee
Gar-dens.' Per-cy Grain-ger wro-ote it." Or: "H-U-M-O-R-E-S-
Q-U-E. That spells 'Humore-esque.' 'Humoresque' was written by Da-vor-zhak!"

To this day I find it impossible to listen to any piece of
music we had to memorize without hearing one of those awful
little tunes in my head. It ruined classical music for me for
years.

We also learned popular songs in Music Appreciation, but
we were so pissed off by the whole method of teaching that we
sometimes improvised our own lyrics. At Lafayette High, Irving Berlin's "Easter Bonnet" started like this: "In your Pass-
over bonnet, with all the matzoh on it . . ."

We also had to learn public speaking. There were two basic
rules of public speaking, we were told: never, never use your
hands, and never look at anyone in the audience. Never use
your hands: if you were Jewish or Italian, that meant you
couldn't talk. It's that sort of lesson in public speaking which
has created terror in the hearts of most people who ever have
to face an audience.

For the most part, I generally muddled along. However, I
did so poorly during my first semester of high school, as did
Herbie, that we were both transferred from the academic program to what was called the general class, or G class. This
was one time when I was cool and Herbie was shaken up. I
really didn't care about school, but Herbie wanted to go to
college—his sister had graduated from college when she
was 18—so Herbie's parents were not too pleased with this
turn of events.

Our homeroom teacher in G class was a man named Mr.
Kilgore. Now, Mr. Kilgore had some sort of notion that he was
our "capo." He thought we were hoodlums, and that only he

could handle us. He used to tell us repeatedly that he had straightened out many wayward boys. Wayward boys. Our crime had been to get a 60 in Geography.

Mr. Kilgore demanded absolute order and obedience and would have a fit if he didn't get it. Our homeroom period began at 8:05 exactly, and we had all better be in our seats on the dot. One day, however, the little hand was on the 8 and the big hand was on the 5, but there was no Mr. Kilgore at the head of the classroom. We waited a few minutes; then at 8:08 we decided to lock the door. At 8:10, Mr. Kilgore showed up and found he couldn't get into the room. He tried the door a few times with his shoulder, then started yelling through the window in the door for us to let him in. We all shook our heads and pointed to our ears, letting him know we couldn't hear him. He kept banging and yelling, and we kept gesticulating. Finally someone put a note up on the door saying that we couldn't hear him. Then someone wrote another note saying that we weren't allowed to leave our seats until Mr. Kilgore dismissed us—pretending that we didn't know the man at the door was Mr. Kilgore. After a few more minutes of this, we decided to let him in so we wouldn't all get permanent detention. When Mr. Kilgore finally walked into the classroom he was, to put it mildly, pissed.

"Who did it? Who locked the door?" he yelled at us. "If whichever little bastards are responsible for this don't speak up, you're all going to be punished!"

He kept bellowing, and we just sat there like angels, until Mr. Kilgore realized he wasn't going to get anywhere with that approach. So he decided he'd change from bad cop to good cop. This is an amusing routine to watch when the bad cop and the good cop are the same person.

"Guys. I'm sorry I yelled at you," he purred. "If you tell me who did it, you won't be punished. I was just so impressed with your cleverness that I just want to know so I can appreciate the joke better." Still not a sound from us. "Fellows, here's what

I'm going to do. I've got a petition here. Whoever was involved in locking the door should sign it, so I know who those very clever fellows are. Larry, here—you take the petition around to your classmates."

On top of this piece of paper Mr. Kilgore had written: "*I admit to locking the door on Mr. Kilgore.*" I took the petition and went over to the kid at the first desk in the room, who happened to be Herbie.

"Larry, why don't you sign it for me?" Herbie said.

I didn't know exactly why he wanted me to do that, but I signed his name to the petition in my best Palmer Method script. I took it to the next kid and he said the same thing, so I signed it for him. After I took it to about eight kids, and signed it for them all, Mr. Kilgore asked me to bring the petition to him.

"Now I've got you, you bastards!" he said. "You are going to pay for this."

"Excuse me, Mr. Kilgore," Herbie said. "I didn't sign that petition."

"What do you mean, you didn't sign it? Your name's right here."

"I didn't sign it. I think if you look, you'll see all the signatures look alike."

Then all the kids to whom I had taken the petition said, Yeah, I didn't sign it—Larry signed it. Instead of getting madder, Mr. Kilgore sort of shrank; he was defeated. After that episode, he never really bothered us too much again. Fortunately, by the end of the semester, Herbie's and my grades had improved enough so that we got to go back into the academic program.

SCHOOL WAS SOMETHING that was *there.* But I didn't consider it my real life. Real life was hanging around with the guys. And one of the greatest adventures of my youth came about through some idle conversation on the corner with some friends.

It was a Monday evening in November 1951. We were all about 17 years old, and as usual we were standing on the corner talking. Part of the ethic of the corner was that you got there as soon as you could after dinner. Being first on the corner was very important, because then you got the lamppost, and the first guy at the lamppost had something to lean against. The second guy there at least could get a hand in; so could the third guy. But if you were fourth or fifth, you really blew it.

On this particular Monday night in November, Sandy Koufax, Herbie Cohen and I were gathered around the lamppost discussing one of the major topics of the day, which was our preferences for various brands of ice cream. Herbie was a big Breyer's man. I liked Borden's. Sandy favored Carvel.

Sandy happened to mention that he had been in New Haven, Connecticut, with his stepfather a couple of weeks earlier and they had stopped at a Carvel where he had actually been given three scoops of ice cream for 15 cents.

This immediately started a violent argument, with Sandy insisting he did get three scoops for 15 cents and Herbie and me arguing that that was impossible. Finally we decided to bet Sandy. Herbie bet $5 and I bet $3 that one could not get three scoops for 15 cents. Naturally, the only way to settle the bet was to go from Brooklyn to New Haven. Herbie had a car, so we went back to his place and got into the car, and then we realized we could not possibly make this trip without Bernie.

Off we drove to Bernie's house. When we walked in, Bernie was just sitting down to dinner with his parents, Dora and Nathan, and we walked in and asked Bernie if he would like to go to Carvel with us. Of course, we did not mention that the Carvel we planned to go to was in New Haven. In New York

City alone there were about two hundred Carvels, with one two blocks from Bernie's house.

Bernie looked at his father and mother and said, "Mother and Father, here is what I am going to do. I am going to go with Sandy and Larry and Herbie. I'm going to Carvel, and since we're having dairy anyway, it's no big deal. I'll just have a little ice cream and I'll be right back."

Bernie got into the car with us and we started off toward Carvel, saying nothing to Bernie about where this Carvel was located. We went down the Belt Parkway to the Brooklyn–Battery Tunnel. All this way Bernie has said nothing about our route. We were all just talking about sports and school and other usual topics. From the Brooklyn–Battery Tunnel to the West Side Highway. The West Side Highway to the Major Deegan Expressway. Off the Deegan Expressway and onto the Merritt Parkway, where the signs said CONNECTICUT and MASSACHUSETTS. This was before the days of interstate highways, so by this time it was about nine-thirty. As we hit the Merritt Parkway, Bernie leaned forward and tapped Herbie on the shoulder and said, "I hate to interrupt this fascinating conversation you're having about football. But I was looking at my watch, and I seem to recall that about three hours ago you three came to my house and said, 'Hey, Bernie, want to go to Carvel?' And I said, 'Hey, Mother, I'm going over to Carvel and I'll be right back.'

"Now, I don't want to be rude; I don't want to be out of place. But I would like to know where the hell we are going."

So Herbie said, "Bernie, Sandy says there's a Carvel in New Haven that serves three scoops for 15 cents."

Bernie said, "That's impossible, Sandy, and I'll bet you all the money in the world that it doesn't serve three scoops for 15 cents."

Bernie forgot all about his mother and father, and now he's anxious to get to Carvel because he has a bet riding on this thing. After about another hour we pulled into New Haven, and New Haven was experiencing an unexpected and very early snowfall.

There we were driving around New Haven at eleven o'clock at night during a snowfall, looking for a Carvel. Finally Sandy spotted the place, and naturally the guy was closing up for the night. Selling ice cream at 11 P.M. during a snowfall is not the most lucrative business practice.

As we pulled up, Herbie said, "Wait a minute. We can't all get out of this car and go in. This guy might know Sandy, and this whole thing could be a setup. Larry, you get out and just order 15 cents' worth and see how many scoops you get."

I got out of the car, went into the Carvel, put my 15 cents on the counter and said, "Chocolate, please." Sure enough, I got three scoops, and we all lost the bet to Sandy. I went back to the car, and we decided to make sure the evening wasn't a total loss, and since this place offered such value, we decided to eat this guy out of Carvel's.

The four of us went back in, and we were really packing those ice creams in. Bernie figured if he ate fourteen of them he'd come out almost even. There we were, stuffing down ice cream, and the owner said to us, "Hey, guys, I don't want to interrupt or anything. I know it's none of my business—but I am having my best night since July fourth, only now it's November and it's snowing."

So we told the guy the whole story of the 15 cents, and it's impossible, and how we had come from Brooklyn just to prove that Sandy was wrong. Now, this guy found it hard to believe that four kids would drive from Brooklyn just to eat ice cream at his place, but what he found more incredible was that he was giving away an extra scoop, because no one at Carvel had told him you don't get three scoops for 15 cents.

Midnight rolled around, and the guy wanted to close up, and we figured we had eaten about as many gallons as we could hold, so we got back into the car. Just to absolutely ensure that the evening was not a total loss, we decided we might as well take a tour of New Haven. Sandy, who had been there with his father, was leading this expedition. He was directing us down this street and that, and it being midnight in the snow, things were pretty much deserted. We turned down a fairly small block, and all of a sudden cars were pulling out in front of us, cars were behind us, people were coming out of buildings with signs and stickers and bumper stickers, and they were plastering all the cars, including Herbie's. A guy actually climbed onto Herbie's car with a huge sign and attached it to the car with a rope.

At that point Bernie said, "Do you think we ought to inquire as to what this occurrence is about?" Through the snow we could make out that all the signs said, "VOTE FOR MAYOR LEE." What was going on was that on Tuesday elections were going to be held in New Haven, and it was illegal to electioneer on election day, so all the campaign workers were making one last effort, and then they were going to a rally for Mayor Lee at the New Haven High School. I have to digress here and explain that about eleven years later I was working in Miami, and Mayor Richard Lee, who was Mayor of New Haven for sixteen years, was in town for a conference and came on the show, and he remembered the whole incident. Anyway, we had ended up in the middle of a parade on the way to the high school. Another digression: Herbie left the MAYOR LEE sign on his car for a month after we got back. The New York City mayoral election was three weeks after New Haven's, and in our Brooklyn district Mayor Lee got 73 write-in votes.

Back to the rally. Being in the mood we were in, the four of us decided to follow all the people and find out what was going on. There must have been four hundred people at the high school, and everyone was having a good time. They were

handing out free coffee and doughnuts for the campaign workers, and we figured, What a bargain. We've lost our bet with
Sandy, and we've already had a lot of Carvel, but free food is
free food; so we were stuffing it in. The four of us were wan-
dering around, eating, having a great time when Sandy came
over to me and said, "Larry, do you know what Herbie is telling everyone about you?" I didn't, so Sandy continued: "Herbie is going around telling everyone what a great campaign
worker you were, and what an important part of the race you
were." None of us even knew what Mayor Lee looked like. But
what the hell. So I went around and told everybody what a
sensational job Herbie had done for Mayor Lee.

Up on the stage in the auditorium were a little speaker's
stand and a few chairs. One was for Mayor Lee, who was going
to thank all the workers, and while we were waiting for Mayor
Lee to show up, the campaign chairman came over to Herbie
and me and said, "I've heard so much about you tonight, how
hard both of you worked, that we would like the two of you to
share the stage with the Mayor as an example of youth in politics." I looked at Herbie, and he looked at the campaign chairman and said, "That would be a great honor, sir." And the two
of us went up and sat down on stage.

There we were, in an auditorium of four hundred strangers
and Sandy and Bernie. At that point Sandy collapsed laughing.
He was on the floor, out of control—and at that moment
something happened to Sandy. Well, let me put it this way: his
mother had a hard time removing the stain from his pants. He
was laughing so hard that he stuffed four doughnuts into his
mouth so he wouldn't make so much noise. Bernie, on the
other hand, was oblivious to the entire thing and thought for
some reason we belonged on stage. So he just waved and called
out, "Hi, Larry; hi, Herbie." He also proceeded to put twenty-
eight doughnuts into his jacket pockets. Bernie figured that by
the end of this trip, even though he agreed to pay $5 for the

bet to Sandy, he would end up $3 ahead on coffee and dough-
nuts and the extra scoops of Carvel.

This was the scene: Herbie and I were on stage. Four hundred people were watching us. Sandy was on the floor peeing in
his pants, and Bernie was waving hello. While we were there,
Herbie beckoned to the campaign manager and suggested that
I introduce Mayor Lee. So the campaign manager introduced
me as one of the mayor's fine young supporters. I stood up—
17 years old, I've never seen Mayor Lee in my life, four hundred people watching, Sandy on the floor and Bernie waving. I
said, "Ladies and gentlemen, I've been asked to introduce the
Mayor. But I think there is someone who deserves that honor
more: my friend Herbie Cohen." I turned to Herbie, and Herbie stood up and did twenty-five minutes.

Herbie did the history of America, Herbie did Paul Revere,
Herbie did the Constitution. Herbie whipped the crowd into a
frenzy. Then he said, "I give you not just the next mayor of
New Haven, but the next United States Senator, the next Governor of Connecticut, the next President of the United States:
Richard Lee." The crowd went wild. Mayor Lee thanked Herbie, then gave his speech, and by the time the whole thing was
over it was two o'clock in the morning.

As the crowd cleared out, Mayor Lee spotted the four of us
in a corner and said, "Fellows, can I talk to you for a minute,
please?" He even asked his campaign manager to wait outside;
he just wanted to talk to the four of us alone. The campaign
manager left, and the Mayor waited for the whole auditorium
to empty. The lights were out, and just the moon was shining
into the hall, and the four of us were standing with Mayor
Lee. Mayor Lee looked at Herbie and me and said, "Fellows,
what I'm going to say now is probably going to break your
hearts. It hurts me to even say it. But if I didn't say it, I
couldn't live with myself. I just couldn't go on; it would
drive me crazy."

"Go ahead, Mayor: say it," Herbie said.

"Well, this may discourage you from politics forever; you may never believe in another politician."

"Mayor, please, say it," Herbie repeated.

"All right. Fellows, I've lived in New Haven all my life. I have four campaign headquarters, and I visit all four of them every day and I have been for two months. Tonight I heard about how hard you fellows worked stuffing envelopes and delivering packages. But I've got to tell you the truth: I've never seen either of you before in my life."

"We've never seen you before either, Mayor," Herbie said.

"We wouldn't know you if we passed you on the street," Bernie threw in. "We don't know you, and we are in this whole place by accident."

The Mayor looked very confused and he asked us where we were from.

"We're from Brooklyn, Mayor," Sandy said.

"Brooklyn. Do you live in New Haven now? Visiting someone in New Haven? Going to college—you're at Yale?"

We, of course, said no to all his questions.

"Well, for goodness' sake, what brought you fellows here?" asked Mayor Lee.

"Well, Mayor. Sandy said there was a Carvel in New Haven that served three scoops for fifteen cents," Herbie explained.

"That's impossible. They can't serve three scoops for fifteen cents," said Mayor Lee.

We then proceeded to explain the whole story of how we had gotten to New Haven from Brooklyn and ended up at his rally. Finally, we finished our story, got back into the car and drove back to Brooklyn. By the time we got back it was five-fifteen in the morning, and snow was falling in Brooklyn, and we realized that the one thing we had forgotten to do was tell Bernie's parents where we had gone.

We drove down the street to Bernie's house, the snow was

falling and standing in front of the house are Bernie's mother and father. This is Jewish masochism. They cannot sit inside and look out the window: no, they must stand in the snow and let the snow fall on them while they're waiting for their Bernie.

We got out of the car and the four of us were walking toward the house, and Bernie's mother said what every mother has said to a teen-age son: "Ten years. Tonight, Bernard, you took ten years off my life."

Bernie's father took a different approach. He took one hand out of his pocket—the fingers on one of his gloves were missing—he took that hand and approached Sandy, Herbie and me and proceeded to bang each of our chests in turn and said, "Bum, bum, bum, bum. You're a bum, and you're a bum, and you're a bum. You bums took my Bernie away. Bums."

Bernie's mother interrupted and said, "Hold it, Nathan. Perhaps there is an explanation for where Bernard was tonight. Bernard, tell your parents where you were."

"Ma, I went to Carvel," said Bernie.

"Don't lie to me, don't lie to me, Bernard!" she said. "When it got to be eight o'clock and you weren't back I made Nathan put on his galoshes and we walked to the Carvel, and I said, 'Where's my Bernie?' and the manager said, 'Your Bernie ain't been here all night.' So where did you go?"

"We went to Carvel, but we didn't go to the Carvel here. We went to another Carvel," Bernie said.

"Where?"

"In New Haven."

"Another ten years, Bernard. You have just taken another ten years from your mother's life!"

Now everyone was screaming and yelling, and lights were going on in the neighborhood and people were looking out of their buildings. Then Bernie's father grabbed Herbie by the chest, pulled the clothes right up to his nose and said, "What the hell did you go to New Haven for?"

"Well, Sandy said there was a Carvel in New Haven that served three scoops for fifteen cents."

And at five-thirty in the morning, in the snow, on a stoop in Brooklyn, Bernie's father said, "That's impossible. They can't serve three scoops for fifteen cents."

PART IV

Early Years

AFTER HIGH SCHOOL GRADUATION, while most of my friends were going to college, I was working at a series of odd jobs—mostly delivery boy and mail-room clerk. Whenever people asked me what I was going to do with my life, I told them I wanted to be on the radio. But I hadn't a clue as to how to go about it. The closest I came was working as mail boy in the Associated Merchandising building, which also housed radio station WOR. I used to ride up to the top floor and hold the "OPEN" button of the elevator door and look into the newsroom; I was too shy to even get out of the elevator and introduce myself to anyone there. Today, WOR carries *The Larry King Show.*

Living in New York had its drawbacks for a kid who wanted to go into radio. Because it was the big time, it was a difficult hometown in which to get a start. Finally someone suggested to me that Miami was a good place to begin in broadcasting; it was a town full of kids on the way up and old guys on the way out, and although it was a low-paying town, jobs were always available.

So in 1957, at age 23, I got on a bus and headed south. Maybe because I realized that if I wasn't going to work up the nerve to apply for a radio job in Miami I might as well decide to become a professional mail boy, I started knocking on doors and getting thrown out of a lot of stations, until I got to WAHR, a very small AM station that doesn't even exist anymore. The general manager, Marshall Simmonds, agreed to meet me, and because he liked my speaking voice, he agreed to give me a test. I'd never been before a microphone, so I had no idea if I had any ability to persuade people to listen to me; but I did have a deep, resonant voice—a voice that prompted people to tell me since I was 15 that I'd sound good on radio—so I figured I was qualified for the business.

Marshall had me read a newscast, and said I sounded okay, and told me to hang around the station; someone was bound to quit. So I practically lived at the station for two weeks. I got a little room next to the laundry in the basement of a small hotel which I slept in for about five hours a night. The rest of the time, I watched the disc jockeys and the newsmen and the talk-show hosts. I got coffee and swept the floor at the station. At the end of the two weeks Marshall called me into the office and said I was to be the disc jockey on the 9 A.M.–to–noon show; sure enough, their regular guy had just quit. I figured my two weeks of watching and sweeping was equivalent to a master's degree in journalism, and I told Marshall I was ready to go.

I was unable to sleep that night. At 2 A.M. I returned to the station and sat in the empty studio waiting for 9 A.M. to roll around. At about four in the morning my confidence had waned a little, but I had been watching these guys for two weeks; I knew there wasn't all that much to it.

At 8:30 A.M., Marshall called me into his office and asked me what name I was going to use. I had never considered being anything but Larry Zeiger.

"Zeiger. It's too German, too Jewish. It's not show-business enough," Marshall said.

When I told him I couldn't think of any alternatives, he said, "How about King?" Obviously, I concurred in his choice.

I've never felt that by changing my name I've tried to conceal who I am. Anyone who has listened to me knows that I'm a Jewish kid from Brooklyn. But if I were starting out today, I wouldn't change my name. Anything's a show-business name today.

At 8:50, Marshall escorted me, new name and all, into the studio. He went back to his office, and I sat there waiting for the ON AIR sign to light up.

At 9:00, the theme song of the show, Les Elgart's "Swinging down the Lane," started, the light went on and I faded down the music to utter my first words on the air. Nothing. I couldn't even open my mouth. I brought the music back up, took a deep breath and faded the music down again. Nothing. Up went "Swinging down the Lane." At this point Marshall, who had been listening to this in his office, opened the door of the studio and yelled (The mike wasn't on, so none of the listeners heard him), "This is a communications business. Communicate!" and slammed the door.

Down went "Swinging down the Lane," and this time I managed to open my mouth. I said, "Ladies and gentlemen, you're probably wondering why Les Elgart is doing all that swinging up and down the lane. Well, my name is Larry King, and this is my first day on the air and I'm nervous. I've been fading the music up and down trying to think of something to say, and the general manager just came in here and told me I'd better start talking."

What I did instinctively was take the listeners into the scene with me, which has been something that has worked for me over the course of my career, and after that initial fifteen minutes, I've never had mike fright again.

This is not to say my career was an unblemished series of triumphs. Because WAHR was such a small station, everyone there had had to do all sorts of jobs. One day you were a disc jockey, the next you'd be a newscaster. After I'd been there a little under a year I was assigned to do an 11-to-11:30 P.M. sports show in addition to the morning music show. The sports show was a wrap-up of the day's sporting events, and since we had no tapes, it was a half-hour of me talking about sports. This was no burden because I'd been a sports fanatic since I was a kid and have always had a good head for sports statistics.

After my show an older guy named Sam Gyson had an evening interview show, and I played the commercials and did the intros for him. Sam was a great guy, a funny man and a real pro who'd been around forever.

On this particular night Sam had no guest, he was just going to go on and talk for an hour; most people would die if they had to do that, but Sam was very opinionated and a good storyteller, and he could go on the air and talk for three hours with no problem. Sam was in the station at eleven as I was starting my show. He was waiting in the studio next to mine, and the two rooms were separated by a large window. The only other guy in the station was the engineer, Herb Hersh. Herb was in the control room which looked onto both Sam's studio and mine. I began to do my sportscast, and I was very into it, giving statistics, team standings, my opinion on how the season was going, when I happened to look up at Sam. Sam was sitting there minding his own business, reading the newspaper. He was also stark naked, eating a banana and scratching himself like an ape. I took one look at this and cracked up. I totally lost control. I couldn't get a word out, I was laughing so hard. I signaled to Herb to put on some music or something, but Herb turned to look at Sam himself and fell off his chair laughing, spraining his ankle in the process. So Herb was on the control-room floor, laughing and grabbing his ankle, I was hysterical in my studio and Sam was eating, reading and scratching in his. I couldn't even cut my mike, because Herb handled that, so all the listeners got to hear me laughing like a maniac. I was trying to explain to the listeners why I was cracking up, but I couldn't even get enough control to do that. I tried to think of the worst thing that had ever happened to me, so I thought about my father's death, and that was hysterical. Nothing worked. It was a real panic situation.

One of the people who happened to be listening to this debacle, however, turned out to be Marshall Simmonds, the general manager. Marshall was on his way home from the theater, and he turned on the radio to check out his station and got ten minutes of hysteria. Naturally, he took a detour to the radio station on his way home. He came into the studio and looked at the scene: his engineer on the floor in pain, his talk-show host naked with a banana and his sports announcer hysterical, and he said, "I would have laughed too."

Marshall had a refreshing, dry sense of humor. The next day he said to me, after I apologized profusely, "Now, Larry, that was real communication last night. I told you when you first went on the air that you were going into a great business. I hope last night proved that to you."

ANOTHER GREAT NIGHT in broadcasting occurred when I made my debut on all-night radio. Fortunately, it was not an augury of what was to happen at Mutual. On this particular night I was subbing for the all-night d.j. I was all alone at the station; at this hour they didn't even have an engineer. I was playing records, minding my own business, when I got a call. It was two-thirty in the morning, and a sexy-sounding woman said, "You drive me crazy. I want you." I was not one to pass up any opportunity, so I said, "I don't have to stay much longer." She said, "I want you now." I told her that I got off at 6 A.M., but she said that was no good, because her husband got home from work at six. Then she gave me her address, which was about ten minutes from the station, and said, "You'll figure out a way. I'm waiting."

There I was, caught in a terrible dilemma. I hadn't been on radio that long, and I really didn't want to do anything to ruin my career before it even got started. On the other hand, I was this socially sort of backward Jewish boy from Brooklyn, and no woman had ever said to me, "I want you."

The record I was playing was ending, and when I came back on the air, I said, "Ladies and gentlemen, I have a real thrill for you. You are going to hear the entire *Harry Belafonte at Carnegie Hall* album." It was a two-record set, so I put the thing on, jumped into the car and drove to this woman's house. I walked to her door, and could see her on the porch. She was about 35, wearing a negligee, a very attractive woman. She had WAHR on, and when she came to the door she said, "I knew you'd figure out something." We went to the couch on the porch, I put my arms around her and just as I was about to kiss her on the neck, Harry Belafonte sang, "Down the way where the nights, where the nights, where the nights, where the nights, where the nights . . ." I threw the woman back onto the couch, got into the car, ran three red lights and pulled up to the station. "Where the nights, where the nights, where the nights, where the nights . . ." was coming out of the turntable, and all the lights on the phones were flashing. I straightened out the record and answered the phone and apologized to the callers. The fourth call I got to was an elderly man with a Yiddish accent, and I said Hello, and he said, "Vare da nights, vare da nights, vare da nights . . . You make me crazy vid vare da nights." I said I was really sorry, but there had been a delay in the studio, and then I asked him why he hadn't just changed stations. He said, "I'm an invalid, an a lady comes ta take care a me during da day, an leaves da radio on at nights because I like ta listen ta your station before I fall asleep, but da radio's across da room, so I've just heard sixteen tousand four hunnerd an twenny-two 'vare da nights.' "

To my regret, the woman who incited the whole thing never called back. But since no one in management had been listening to the station at that hour, I considered myself lucky.

AFTER I'D BEEN with WAHR about a year and a half, I got a job offer from WKAT, a larger station in the market. I was perfectly happy at WAHR, but it seemed natural to move to a bigger station which paid more money, so I went. At WKAT, I was thought of as a rising star—a star in a very small constellation, to be sure—and I was given the much-coveted morning drive-time slot.

WKAT was anxious for more attention than it was getting, and consequently the on-air people were given a lot of freedom to develop a personality. It was at WKAT that I really started to find myself and to break away from being a standard disc jockey. I started doing crazy things—interrupting the newscasts, inventing characters. One of my most successful was Captain Wainright of the Miami State Police. I don't do voices that well, but I got a mike amplifier and tried to sound like Broderick Crawford when I did Captain Wainright.

One morning, as Captain Wainright, I interrupted our traffic reporter. Now, traffic reporters have always amused me. If a traffic reporter tells you one route is jammed, and advises taking an alternative route, unless you are the only one listening to the broadcast the alternative route is more than likely to end up as jammed as the original route. So when our traffic reporter finished, I took the microphone as Captain Wainright and said, "This is Captain Wainright, and you commuters have probably noticed that for the past eight months there's been a detour sign on I-95 because they haven't finished the road yet. Well, I want to tell all you folks that the road was finished last night. Ignore that detour sign! Drive right down I-95." Five minutes later I came back on as Captain Wainright and said, "Larry, did you hear my report about I-95? I've got them backed up to Hollandale Boulevard."

As myself, I said, "Captain Wainright, you mean to tell me I-95 is not finished and you sent all those people down an unfinished highway? You can't do that, Captain Wainright."

"Yes I can, Larry. I'm a captain. I can do anything."

One day I interrupted the racing results and said as Captain Wainright, "All you fine folks don't have to bother to go all the way down to the racetrack to get some betting pleasure. Just flag down any of our fine Dade County police officers and place a bet with him."

I had Captain Wainright go into merchandising: "Would you folks like to assure yourselves of never getting a traffic ticket again? For thirty-eight ninety-five—that's right, only thirty-eight ninety-five—you folks can obtain an authentic revolving roof light for your very own car. Just turn this baby on, and no cop will ever stop you again."

Captain Wainright became a total alter ego for me. I had no idea what he was going to say. It was like unleashing another personality; Captain Wainright could get away with anything. Captain Wainright was also responsible for my getting noticed in Miami. The papers began writing him up. Bumper stickers started appearing that read: "DON'T STOP ME. I KNOW CAPT. WAINRIGHT." Dick Gerstein, Miami's State Attorney, who used to get teased by Captain Wainright, called me up, which is how we became friends. I used to do things with Dick like saying, "Dickie baby, where are you? Today is payoff day, and if you're not in the office in five minutes, I'm going to call out the boys."

THE ATTENTION Captain Wainright received led to my first big career break. Pumpernik's, a popular Miami restaurant, wanted to increase its morning business and hit upon the idea of having a radio talk show broadcast out of its dining room. When this was offered me I was 25, and it turned out to be a very heady thing. The format couldn't have been simpler. I sat in front of the big plate-glass window in the dining room and interviewed whoever happened to show up. There was no producer, no booked guests, no plan at all.

The first morning, I interviewed the waitresses. The second morning I interviewed plumbers; there was a plumbers' convention in town. The third morning, I interviewed waitresses and plumbers. The fourth morning, I interviewed Bobby Darin. He had heard the show the morning before and wondered what the hell it was all about and decided to drop by the restaurant. Bobby Darin had just recorded "Mack the Knife," and he was at the hottest point of his career. A few days later, Jimmy Hoffa came on the show: he was in town for a Teamsters' convention.

What made the Pumpernik's show such a breakthrough, and propelled me to one of Miami's largest radio stations, and to television, was that I found I could do more than shtick. I found that I had an ability to draw people out in an interview. The key to my success as an interviewer is in the fact that I am truly interested in a person's craft, in his or her work. And when you sincerely want to find out why people do what they do, and how they do it, you are going to learn a lot.

For example, I enjoyed having those plumbers on, the first few days. Who, as a kid, hasn't been fascinated to watch plumbers or electricians or carpenters at work? Well, Pumpernik's gave me a chance to find out about being a plumber.

One of the plumbers was terrific. He said, "I'm a wonderful person to be around. Plumbers are very candid. Bricklayers are not. Carpenters. Carpenters are earnest." He said that there are natural plumbers, and a plumber can tell just by looking at another plumber's work whether he is a journeyman or an artist. He also said that he can go into someone's house, or a hotel, and tell where they are going to have trouble, and how soon. Sometimes I wish I could go back to that occasionally— to interviewing people who aren't famous. Celebrityhood does not necessarily confer thoughtfulness or eloquence, as any talk-show host can tell you.

One of the "real people" I interviewed during that time turned out to be my biggest challenge as a host. While I was doing the Pumpernik's show, a meeting of World War I and II ace pilots was in Miami, and someone suggested I have on one of World War II's most-decorated aces. This guy had shot down fifteen German planes.

He came to the studio, and we talked off the air for a few minutes about his occupation—the computer business, which was just starting its revolutionary changes. Everything was fine until we went on the air. I started by asking how a fighter pilot ends up in computers.

"There was a job open, and I took it," he said.

"In the computer business, how important is the human being compared with the machine?" I asked.

"Fifty–fifty."

"What made you join the Air Force?"

"I like planes."

This guy, a World War II hero, was absolutely panicked. Sweat was pouring off him. We had fifty-five minutes left of the show, and the guy was absolutely paralyzed. So I decided to use it, just as I had used my own fear my first time on the air.

I said to the ace, "I could never get into a plane and try to shoot down an enemy pilot; I'd be scared to death. But I can tell that you're nervous sitting here having to talk into the mike."

He shook his head in assent. I went on: "Why is it scary to appear on radio, and not scary to fly in enemy territory?" That question led us into a whole discussion of fear. The pilot said that when he was in the cockpit of his plane, he was in control. Whatever went right was his doing, just as whatever went wrong was his doing. But he had no control over the radio show; he had no idea what I was going to do or say. By the end of the show, he was ready to go out on a national tour. The microphone between us had disappeared and we were just two people having a conversation about his life.

Another really tough guest was the physicist Edward Teller, the "father of the H-bomb." Teller was a visiting professor at the University of Miami, and another professor who was a listener persuaded Teller to appear on my TV show—by then I had a late-night television show on the weekend. While he was getting his makeup put on I went in and introduced myself. Teller is a very imposing man; he has a heavy German accent, and enormous bushy eyebrows which he uses to dramatic effect.

"Vat do you know about me?" he asked me.

I told him I knew he had invented the hydrogen bomb, and that he had testified against Robert Oppenheimer, the principal physicist behind the atomic bomb, when Congress was investigating whether Oppenheimer was a security risk.

"Everyvun knows dat. Vat do you know about my contribution to pheeseecs?"

"Nothing," I had to say honestly.

"Den I vill not do dis show," Teller said, pushing away the makeup woman.

I had a half-hour show booked with this guy, and he was

threatening not to do it. I said to him, "Doctor, I will make a deal with you. Let me start the interview, and anytime you're unhappy with it, I promise you, you can get up and walk out, and we will not run any of the tape."

Teller agreed. While we were on the set getting the lighting checked and the microphones set up he refused to say a word to me. The director gave the cue we had a minute to go, and Teller looked at me and said, "By de vay, don't ask me about de H-bomb."

Don't ask about the H-bomb. Great. I figured he'd walk, and we'd have to dig up another guest. Then the red light on the camera went on and I said to Teller, "Why is it that in high school everyone hated to take physics?"

Teller's face lit up. He said it was taught terribly because most high school teachers don't understand physics. "Pheeseecs is life. Dat's vat dey should call it—life, not pheeseecs," he said.

Then I asked him, "Let's say you're designing a nuclear weapon and you're doing all the math and it takes months."

"Years," Teller said.

"All right. You spend years doing the math. And you finally get the math to work. Do you have to go to the test site to make sure it goes off?"

"No. Vonce de mat vorks, de bomb vill work. For example, de H-bomb. De H-bomb has been tested tree times and I've never been dere for any of de tests. Vonce de mat works, de bomb vill work."

At this point we were six minutes into the inteview, and I knew not only that he was going to stay, but that no subject would be off-limits. After all, he had brought up the H-bomb. Not only that, he carried it into a discussion of the effect the bomb had on his life.

"I'm sure you know de H-bomb has never been dropped on a human being," Teller said. "De A-bomb has been dropped twice. Einstein helped invent a bomb dat killed two million people. Dey don't call heem de 'fodder of de A-bomb.' Dey call me de 'fodder of de H-bomb' and de H-bomb never killed anyvun."

Then I asked him about the image of a mad scientist. How did it feel to have people talk about him that way?

"You haf to be a little mad to be infolfed in changing tings; infentors, creative people, change tings," he said.

When the interview ended, he put his arm around me and said, "Vy didn't you tell me you knew so much apout pheeseecs?" And I explained to him that I had been a terrible student and I really didn't know anything about physics, but someone who knew a lot about physics wouldn't have thought to ask the questions I'd asked.

As MUCH AS I LIKED doing the Captain Wainright stuff, and enjoy the shtick on the Mutual show today, I found that the interviews I did on the Pumpernik show not only gave a boost to my career, but gave me a new way of looking at myself. Part of my approach in interviews was that of the kid from Brooklyn who was getting an education through his guests. And I found that listeners were learning something too. Of course, it wasn't all serious. Two regular guests on the Pumpernik show were an unknown comic named Don Rickles and cult figure Lenny Bruce.

Rickles worked the Miami clubs and was by no means a recognizable face in those days. He used to come in dressed as a busboy and go through the restaurant insulting the customers. Then at the end of the show he would join me and do a critical, and I mean critical, review of the entire show.

He started to catch on, and then went to California and became a big hit on the Dean Martin show. A few years later he was back in Miami working at one of the big resorts and I called him up and asked him to be on my show. By this time Don didn't take his own calls, but when I gave my name to his secretary, Don got on the phone:

"Larry, I know what you're going to say, Larry. You knew me when, is that it? You knew me when and now you want me to do your show. Larry, I'm a very big person now. They screen my calls for me, Larry. I don't need your show now, Larry. I let them put you through because I didn't want to look like a snob now that I'm big. So why don't you put it a different way? Say: 'I need your help, Don.' "

During this whole monologue I had not uttered one word, but if I learned anything at Pumpernik's, it was don't try to top Don Rickles. So I said, "I need your help, Don."

"What do you want from me, Larry?"

"I want you to do my show, Don."

"No, no, no. Say: 'I want you to do my show so my show will be famous.' "

And he had me repeating all this stuff after him; but he did come on the show, and he was wonderful.

Lenny Bruce had the most brilliant comic mind I'd ever encountered. Of course, he was victimized by law-enforcement officials who felt their highest duty was to protect adults from being able to pay to hear the comic of their choice at a nightclub. But if he hadn't been hounded mercilessly by police and prosecutors, I don't know that Lenny would have had a happy life; he had a very strong self-destructive streak.

It was breathtaking to listen to Lenny. When he appeared on the show, he did very little prepared material. He was able to let the most mundane things spark incredible flights of invention.

Once he came into Pumpernik's wearing an entire, authentic prison uniform. The microphones were set up in front of a large plate-glass window, and Lenny sat down and pointed out the window and said, "Keep your eye on the cop." Lenny explained that a friend had given him the prison uniform, and as he approached the restaurant he had decided to stop a cop and ask him for directions. Well, the cop was standing right near Pumpernik's window, and Lenny began doing a description of what was going through the cop's head:

"Now, here's this stark human dilemma. The cop looks like he's about twenty-seven years old. And the first thing he thinks is, 'Prisoner. I'm going to call in. But then I'll look like a jerk; why would a prisoner wear a prison uniform and talk to a cop? They'll all laugh at me.' Now, watch: our boy is forgetting the whole thing and directing traffic. Wait—he's looking troubled again. Now he's thinking, 'Wait a minute. Suppose this is a genius prisoner who has escaped and is wearing his uniform, figuring no cop is going to call in to check on a guy wearing a uniform . . .' "

Then Lenny would do a whole monologue on deceit, and how to get away with doing something you're not supposed to do:

"You know the best way to cheat with a girl? You want to cheat with a girl, man, you walk right into the front lobby with her and take her onto the elevator. Six thousand people are watching you, and no one thinks you're doing anything wrong. You want to get caught: hide in the back of the car and drive to the Kozy Korner Motel and duck down at the red lights, and your wife will be at the front desk getting a pack of cigarettes when you pull up. No, the right way to do it: prance right through the front lobby of a motel, call your wife and say, 'Hi. I'm in room 627 with Darlene Burns and we are about to ball our heads off.' And she'll say, 'Ha-ha, Lenny, you're very funny. Now stop kidding around; I've got things to do.' "

Lenny was a great interview in a way, because all I had to do was ask him one thing and he could do the rest of the show by himself. Of course, he could be difficult if I was actually trying to get him to answer more than one question. I've never met anyone with instincts like Lenny's, though. I remember I asked him once who was the funniest man in the world. He said, "George Gobel." Upon hearing that, anyone would think, "George Gobel? the funniest man in the world?" but that's exactly why Lenny said it. He explained, "You see, if I said Milton Berle, you'd say, 'Oh, yeah, that makes sense. Milton Berle is very funny.' And if I said Pinky Lee, you'd say, 'Oh, come on, Lenny, you're kidding.' But George Gobel, you just don't know. Now, it must be tough to be George Gobel, because he is funny, but he's nobody's favorite comedian. So George Gobel is my favorite comedian."

From time to time, Lenny and I would drive around Miami in the afternoon, just talking. He was a guy who did not like to be alone; he was always before an audience, even if it was only one person. Once he told me about getting into trouble while he was performing in San Francisco: he got arrested for saying a dirty word. The word was "cocksucker," which is still dirty today, but you're not going to get arrested for saying it. I remember his saying, in regard to his own troubles, that people would be nude on Broadway by 1970. He was right except for one thing: it happened a lot sooner than 1970. Anyway, he was working in a club and he used the word, and two cops were in the audience—there were cops at a lot of his performances; they knew he would say something "obscene" and they could bust him, and the D.A. could take credit for cleaning up smut—and Lenny got busted. Lenny said, "So I said 'cocksucker' and the two cops put me in the squad car and drove me down to night court; it was a misdemeanor, so I would get an immediate hearing at night court, and one of the cops says to me, 'What did you say that word for?' And I said to him, 'Anyone ever do it to you?' And the cop said, 'No, the wife don't believe in it.' At this point the second cop said to his partner, 'You shitting me, man?—you never do it?' I'm sitting in the back seat listening to them have a discussion of the word I'm being dragged to court for. Finally, we get to court and the judge asks what the charge is, and the first cop says using lewd and lascivious language in a public place. The judge says, 'What did he say?' and the cop says, 'I can't repeat it in an open courtroom.' There are about two hundred people in the courtroom—some of the court appearances were better than the club dates—and I pointed out that the judge couldn't rule unless he knew what the word was, so the cop whispers, ' "Cocksucker." ' The judge says, 'I didn't hear you.' The cop says 'cocksucker' again, but a little louder this time. The judge says, 'Cocksucker?'—which puts the whole court into an uproar. So since the judge and the cop have said it, I charged the whole court with using lewd and lascivious language in a public place, and they dismissed the charges."

THE PUMPERNIK SHOW became a must-do for visiting celebrities. Danny Thomas came by, Ella Fitzgerald, Ed Sullivan. I also had non–show-business guests. One was Hubert Humphrey. He was one of the warmest men I've ever met; you couldn't help liking him. Goldwater once said that Humphrey's gift was that he was so American. I had Humphrey as a guest on several of my shows over the years, once while he was the Vice President; this was during the Vietnam war, and he was the recipient of a lot of hostility. My first question to him was "Do you ever miss pharmacy?" He was really thrown by that: He had been expecting something on the order of *Meet the Press*. I'm sure no one had brought up pharmacy with him since the 1948 convention. He said to me that it was very strange that I asked that question: about a month earlier he had been back in Minnesota and decided to spend the day filling prescriptions in his father's drugstore. No press or photographers were there; he just went in and went behind the counter. "You know what amazed me?" he said. "Ninety-two percent of the prescriptions I filled were for a drug I'd never filled in my life: Valium. You can learn a lot about people from filling prescriptions. And here I was in this corner drugstore in Minneapolis—the comfortable Midwest, not New York City—and almost all the prescriptions were for tranquilizers. I'm not saying this is a bad thing; perhaps this drug was helping many many people who used to have to suffer in the past; but I still thought it said a lot about society today."

The fact that I started with pharmacy does not mean we didn't discuss Vietnam; but I'm not *Meet the Press,* and I think there's room for a lot of different styles of interviewing, and I think what I do best is create a sense of intimacy and comfort for the guest, and in that way the audience can learn a lot about the guest's character and beliefs.

I also asked Richard Nixon a question no one had ever asked before and got a surprising answer. I had Nixon on the air several times during the sixties. He was out of office at that time, but obviously interested in running for the presidency again. In 1966 he was doing my Miami TV show. We had talked several times about the past, and particularly about his debate with Kennedy during the 1960 campaign. I said to him, "You and John Kennedy came to Congress as freshmen in the same year. Did you ever debate Kennedy before the presidential campaign?" He said that in fact, they had:

"When the Taft-Hartley Law was proposed in 1948, the Rotary Club of Harrisburg, Pennsylvania, sent a request to the Republican congressional leadership and the Democratic congressional leadership asking for two congressmen to come and debate the bill," he said. "John Kennedy and I were picked. It was a morning debate, so we both took the overnight train from Union Station. We were in the same sleeping compartment, so we flipped a coin to see who would get the upper and who would get the lower berth. I lost and slept in the upper berth, and Kennedy beat me ever since."

In typically Nixonian fashion, however, he had to add a postscript to what was a charming story by saying he had gotten more applause at the debate in Harrisburg.

Nixon never aroused the hatred in me that he does in so many people. He could be an excellent guest: very insightful, conversant with the world situation. If I were the President, I would want Nixon to be my Secretary of State. First of all, he loves foreign affairs, and he gets along with other heads of state; he gets along with them much better than he gets along with other Americans. And if he is not a problem solver himself, he is a marvelous analyst. But even when he was on the show and things were low-key and relaxed, that Nixon paranoia would come through. For example, he was on a radio show with me in 1965 and had been in very good form as we went to commercial break. There were three technicians in the control room, and they were talking among themselves during the break, and Nixon leaned over to me and said, "You see those three guys?" I said I did. "They're talking about me," he said. I was really taken aback. I asked him how he knew they were. "I can sense it," he said. It was that quality of Nixon's that really did him in. So what if the guys in the control room were talking about him?—and it was more likely they were discussing baseball. The paranoia became such an overwhelming quality that it sabotaged some very good qualities he has. In a small social setting he can be an excellent host, quite sociable, and a good listener. Very few politicians are really good listeners.

One politician who didn't want to hear any questions that might interfere with his prepared act was George Wallace. I had him on my television show in 1968 when he was running for the presidency and was at the height of his power. Now, even when I disagree with someone, and George Wallace's philosophy couldn't be more inimical to mine, I always try to be respectful and avoid confrontation. You probably learn more about a host than about a guest during a confrontational encounter. But Wallace drove me closer to losing my temper than any other guest I've ever had. The show was just beginning, and I introduced Wallace, and he looked around the studio and said, "I don't see any Negroes here." I said, "They own the station, but they're on their lunch break." Then I said to him, "You have often said that it is none of government's business if a businessman—let's say a restaurateur—doesn't want to serve someone. Now, suppose when you were Governor, you were walking down the street in Miami and a black man who had lost his leg in Vietnam came up to you and said, 'Governor, I can't eat in a restaurant on Main Street.' How would you answer that man?" Wallace said, "When you're Governor you've got no time to be walking down the street chitchatting." That answer was a total evasion, but we had to break for commercial before I could call him on it. During the commercial he leaned over to me and said, "Keep it up: this is great television." At that point I lost all respect for him. I hold no brief for racists, but Wallace as much as admitted to me that he laid it on extra thick for theatrical purposes. When we came back I started grilling him about foreign relations, economics, the Social Security system. He was stumbling all over the place because I wouldn't let him answer with his pat phrases, and it showed he hardly had the breadth of knowledge to be President.

Several years later I had him on the show again, after he was reelected Governor, and his attitude toward race had toned down a lot; he even had blacks on his staff. I asked him about it—why things had changed. He said, "I took a look at the registration sheets. They're voting."

*   *   *

IN 1962 I got an offer to join WIOD, one of the biggest radio stations in town. The WIOD management loved the Pumpernik show, the spontaneity of it, and wanted a similar show, in the evening, for themselves, so I made the switch. There had recently been a popular television detective show called *Surfside 6* which was filmed partly in Miami. In it the fictional detective, whose phone exchange was Surfside 6, lived on a houseboat docked along the beach. It was decided to move the location of my show from a restaurant to this houseboat. The houseboat move was a masterly stroke of p.r.—it was good publicity for the television show and for our show. And because we were docked right there on the beach with a speaker set up on shore, we became quite an evening attraction.

The *Surfside 6* show was even bigger than the Pumpernik's show, and the location had a lot to do with it. Even though the listeners couldn't see the setting, the casualness, the party atmosphere came through. As at Pumpernik's, people who were in town performing would simply drop by unannounced. And when you're floating on the water late at night and having fun, people really tend to drop their guard. I remember one night I was interviewing Ed Sullivan while Alan Alda was in the galley pouring himself a glass of milk—it was that sort of show. Alda was not at all well known at that time; he was simply Robert Alda's son. Often when he was in town performing at the Coconut Grove Playhouse he'd come by after the performance and sit around and talk.

Alda was exactly then as he comes across now: sincere, politically committed, very caring and madly in love with his wife. There's not a phony bone in his body. I remember he much preferred talking about politics to discussing show business.

And he was not at all sure he was ever going to really make it in the business, but he felt he had to keep plugging for a while yet. Once Alene and I flew up to New York to see Alan in a play on Broadway. Afterward he and his wife joined us and we all went out for dinner. It's funny to think now about how we walked down those crowded Manhattan streets and not a soul recognized Alan Alda.

Another show-business person better known then for his relationship to a star than for his own talent whom I got to know fairly well was Elliott Gould. At that time he was "that actor who's married to Barbra Streisand." While he was appearing at the Coconut Grove Playhouse he became an unofficial co-host of the show for a week. I've seen Elliott on television in subsequent years, and he seems as if he's just arrived from another planet, but back in the sixties when I knew him he was very sharp and very funny. He did a wonderful shtick about Barbra Streisand's mother—"the ultimate Jewish mother," he called her. He said being married to Barbra meant being married to her mother. Typical observations by Elliott's mother-in-law included, according to Elliott: "I don't understand why you want to be in show business when you're married to one of the greatest talents in the business. You'd be better off becoming her manager." "Why did you get Barbra a blue sweater? You know she looks much better in red." "I hope you realize how lovely Barbra is. There'll never be another Barbra. You're a very lucky boy to be married to such a star."

It's funny how fortunes change in show business. A few years before Elliott Gould came on the show, I had Barbra Streisand as a guest, but at that time she was as unknown as her husband. A friend from one of the hotels called me and asked me to have her on: he was desperate to drum up more business for her. He said he'd seen this kid perform in New York and booked her for the hotel, but she was bombing; no one was showing up. I had her on the show. She didn't sing, so

I had no idea how talented she was; we just talked about her hopes for her career. She was very self-confident, almost arrogant. I asked her about her nose—why she didn't have it fixed. She said she had no desire to look like Doris Day.

I really didn't think too much about her, and didn't expect to hear of her again. She eventually wound up buying back her contract from the hotel so she wouldn't be forced to work for only $3,000 a week.

Although creative people—musicians, writers, dancers, artists—can be difficult to interview—they often have a hard time putting into words exactly how they do what they do—I've always been fascinated by the creative process and enjoy talking to artists of all kinds. Once I had the great pianist and composer Erroll Garner on the show. Garner was not an educated man—I'm not sure he even finished grade school, and he didn't even know how to read music—but he was a musical genius. After he started to relax, he talked with great insight about what he did. He said that melodic structure just ran through him; music was in his head all the time. Then he told the story of how he came to write one of his songs.

He and a friend were driving somewhere and Garner was humming a tune, and his friend said, "What is that? That's a beautiful melody." Garner said it was some song he'd heard on the radio or something; he'd been humming it for years. The friend asked to hear it again, so Garner hummed it for him. The friend, who was a musician himself, said he'd never heard the tune before. Garner assured him it was some old song— after all, the melody had been buzzing around in his head for years. Finally, after extensive discussion, Garner's friend convinced him that there was no such song, and told Garner to put down the tune on paper. He later titled it "Misty." And he admitted he never would have written that classic if his friend hadn't browbeaten him into it.

*   *   *

BECAUSE THE *Surfside 6* show was so casual, friends of mine as well as performers in town dropped by frequently. One regular was jockey Bill Hartack. As I've noted, Bill is a charming man, but one of variable moods. One evening I was interviewing the actor Franchot Tone when Bill came by. Bill was in one of his feisty moods that night, and after about ten minutes with Franchot Tone, Bill said to me during the commercial, "You know, this is an easy job you have, sitting around talking to people."

"If it's so easy, why don't you do it?" I replied.

At that point we came back from commercial, and I said, "Ladies and gentlemen, my friend the distinguished jockey William Hartack claims it takes no skill to be an interviewer, and to prove it, he is going to continue the conversation with Franchot Tone." I turned the microphone over to Bill and left the boat and went to an ice cream parlor. I came back twenty minutes later to find Franchot Tone interviewing Hartack about what it's like to be a jockey.

One of the tenderest nights on the show occurred by chance. It was about midnight, and whoever the scheduled guest had been had left and I was sitting there talking to Hartack when the producer handed me a note saying that Joe Di-Maggio, Jr., had been walking by the houseboat and had seen the sign for the show and wondered if he could come in. I said sure. The young DiMaggio was about 25, and I thought he and Bill could talk a little about sports. For some reason, something clicked with DiMaggio, and he started talking about being his father's son, and about Marilyn Monroe, and it was an incredibly poignant experience.

"I never knew my father," he said. "My parents were divorced when I was little, and I was sent away to private school, and my father was totally missing from my childhood. When they needed a picture of father and son, I'd get picked up in a limo and have my picture taken. We were on the cover of the first issue of *Sport* magazine when it came out in 1949, my father and I, me wearing a little number 5 jersey. I was driven to the photo session, we had the picture taken and I was driven back. My father and I didn't say two words.

"I cursed the name Joe DiMaggio, Jr. At Yale I played football—I deliberately avoided baseball—but when I ran out on the field and they announced my name, you could hear the crowd murmur. . . . When I decided to leave college and join the Marines, I called my father to tell him. You call your father when you make that sort of decision. So I told him, and he said, 'The Marines are a good thing,' and there was nothing more for us to say to each other."

DiMaggio, Jr., said that the closest he'd ever been to his father was in the car on the way to Marilyn Monroe's funeral. He said his father had always gone on loving Monroe, and that he loved her too. She was the one who would call Joe, Jr., to talk, and they kept in touch after the divorce. "My father was crying all the way to the funeral, and he was in so much pain that he reached out and held my hand all the way there. It was the closest I've ever been to him."

The intimacy of the atmosphere on the boat had its effect not only on the guests; it had the same effect on women. The guy who owned the boat worked on it during the day: he was a yacht salesman; but he told me that anytime I wanted to stay over, the place was mine. I had an apartment in Miami, but there was nothing like spending the night docked on a fabulous houseboat. I'd like to think it's my charm and matinee-idol good looks that brought women flocking to me; but obviously the key was that I was a visible person in a "glamorous" profession. People in the public eye are constantly having to deal with the problem of deciding who is sincerely interested in you, and who is interested in knowing a celebrity. During my years in Miami, I never examined this issue too closely; if being a celebrity drew women to me, or got me into circles such as Lou Wolfson moved in, then I saw it as a benefit of being well known. Strangely, that is less of a problem for me today than it was in Miami: I may be a well-known voice, but I'm not a well-known face. I think that many celebrities can protest too much about not being wanted for themselves; very few people are forced into the public eye against their will. And if some intrinsic ability, such as getting people to want to listen to you, is what makes you a celebrity, then that quality should also make people want to be with you when you're away from the radio or television.

Anyway, at the *Surfside 6*, I was reaping the social benefits of the show and not worrying too much about the moral or ethical issues it raised.

ONE NIGHT I was doing the show—I can't even remember whom I was talking to—when a goddess walked by the window. She was alone, and a moment after passing by, she came back to watch the show in progress through the window on the houseboat. She just stood there smiling. A speaker was set up on the deck so passersby could hear the show. I passed a note to the producer that he had to find out who this woman was. He went out and asked if he could help her. She told him she was an actress and a great fan of mine and she wondered if she could watch the show. Could she watch the show? The room we broadcast from was set up with couches, and she sat opposite me on one of the couches. She had dark hair, dark eyes, alabaster skin, a magnificent figure. She was wearing a very short skirt, and she kept crossing and recrossing her legs. I had about a half-hour left of the show, and I was trying to pay attention to it while keeping up silent communication with her. Fifteen minutes before the show finished she started blowing me little kisses, and I started blowing them back. Finally the show ended. The guests cleared out, I indicated to the producer that he could leave immediately and she and I were alone. We talked for a few minutes about her career, about living in Miami, and boom, we were in the bedroom. We spent the night there, and she came back for the next evening's show, after which we also had about five minutes of conversation, and off to the bedroom. We went out once or twice to dinner after that, and then I stopped seeing her. I had the feeling it was not an unusual pattern for her, and it certainly wasn't for me; during that period a two-week affair was a long-term romance.

Two years later, I was the emcee at the opening of an art museum—during that time I did a lot of openings and speaking engagements—and a limo pulled up with one of the richest men in Miami, and she got out of the car with him—which was only natural, since they had gotten married six months before. Now she was on the social committee of the Friends of Animals, chairwoman of fund-raising for the children's hospital, a big hostess. I was standing there with a mike and she and her husband swept by, and I gave her a look that said, "Well, hello there," and she absolutely blanked me out, would not acknowledge she had ever seen me before. She had landed a big catch and did not want to remember her past. At the cocktail reception I went up to her and said sotto voce, "How quickly they forget." She said, in this incredible, phony-upper-crust lockjaw, "Larry, you were absolutely mah-velous tonight. A wonderful emcee. I wonder, are you available—for a fee, of course—to mingle at private parties?" I enjoyed her little act so much that I didn't even try to cut her down. I had to admire her; she had turned whatever theatrical talent she had into a lifetime run.

Another funny experience with a woman happened on the boat. Back in Bensonhurst, as I've indicated, I was not exactly the Burt Reynolds of the neighborhood; I was close to retarded as far as women were concerned. But I did have girlfriends from time to time, and my biggest high school girlfriend was named Fran Golden. Oh, I was crazy about Fran Golden. We went out for about a year when I was 17. Fran was my introduction to sex. Not that we ever even got our clothes off—but most introductions to sex, at least in those days, were of the fumbling, awkward variety that Fran and I had. I hadn't seen Fran since I'd left high school, but one day at the studio I got a message that Fran Golden had called. It had been about ten years since I'd seen her. I called her back and found out she was living in Florida with her husband and three kids, and she'd heard me on the radio and finally gotten up the nerve to call me. I invited her to come by the boat and watch the show. I was terribly nervous the evening she was scheduled to arrive. I had no designs on her, but I wondered how she looked, how she'd think I looked and if there would still be a spark between us. Finally she arrived. She didn't look that different, although she had rather a matronly air, but as soon as she opened her mouth I was floored. "Larrr-y. Oh, Larrr-y, you're so *famous*. I told my children I was going to see a friend of mine who was so *famous*. Larrr-y, you've got to give me your autograph for my kids." All this was delivered in an earsplitting Brooklyn accent. I kept saying to myself, "I would have died for this ten years ago!" I couldn't wait for her to leave so I could stop hearing how famous I was. It's funny—she was probably the same as she'd been in high school. I was the one who had changed.

Part of the reason Fran was so impressed with my fame was that I was also appearing on local television at the time. While I was doing the Pumpernik show I got an offer from one of the stations to do a late-night weekend talk show. About a year after that, one of the biggest stations in town, WTVJ, called me and asked me to do a feature segment for the weekend news. The news thing was sort of a gimmick, but an effective one. I did a regular hour interview with a guest and the station edited it, so that portions of the interview appeared on the six-o'clock and eleven-o'clock news during the weekend. What made it particularly effective was that the station would edit each segment so that it ended just as my guest was telling some interesting story, obliging the viewer to watch the next segment to find out what happened.

Although radio was always my most important outlet, I enjoyed the television work a lot. I was lucky I had a chance to pursue it at all and wasn't pulled after my first night on the air. On my debut show I had on two or three guests and we were all sitting in a semicircle in those swivel chairs that are talk-show standard. I was wound a little tight that night, and during one particularly heated segment of the discussion I tried to get a response from one of the guests. As I turned to address him, I gave the swivel chair a little too much body english and ended up doing an entire 360-degree turn in my chair. For my following show the management provided stationary furniture.

During this period I also—yes, it's hard to believe—got married again. My wife was a lovely woman named Mickey Sutphin. Our major problem was that we had no business being married, as we quickly discovered. We split up after only a few months.

In keeping with the rest of my career, my newspaper column also came about largely through luck. The *Miami Beach Sun* got a new editor around 1965, a guy by the name of Rolf Neal. But before he took over the job, Rolf came and lived in Miami incognito for two months to get the feel of the place, what concerned the citizens—that sort of thing. One thing he felt the *Sun* needed was a columnist with a strong personality. So after two months of hearing me on the radio and seeing me on TV, he offered me a column when he took over the paper.

It was a gamble for us both, but it paid off. I was no William Safire, or Ellen Goodman; mine was an old-fashioned sort of Walter Winchellian column; but I loved doing it, and it got great reader response.

A year or so after I started doing the column for the *Sun*, I spotted John Knight at the racetrack one afternoon. Knight was the founder of the Knight-Ridder newspaper chain, which owned *The Miami Herald*. Knight, who died in 1981, was a very powerful man in Miami. I'm usually not one for introducing myself to strangers, but Knight was one man I wanted to meet, so I went over to him. He couldn't have been more charming, saying he had been listening to me, and reading my column, for quite a while. Buoyed by his recognition, I asked him if he would appear on my television show. Without hesitating he said yes.

That afternoon I told my producer to set something up; John Knight rarely did local shows, and I wanted to make sure he didn't have a chance to change his mind. He did the show a week or so later. We had a couple of other media people on that day, and like so many discussions during the mid-sixties, ours turned to national politics. Knight said that one of the saddest things he was seeing was the vilification of Wayne Morse and Ernest Gruening, the two senators who voted against the Gulf of Tonkin resolution—the resolution that gave Lyndon Johnson the power to step up our involvement in Vietnam. He said they were real heroes, and that any further involvement in Vietnam would turn out to be a terrible thing. Now, this was very early on, before most college students even knew where Vietnam was. Someone else on the panel asked Knight if that meant he thought the American soldiers who had died there had died in vain. At that time we had lost about five thousand men, and we tragically went on to lose ten times that number. Knight thought for a moment and said yes, perhaps it would turn out they had died for nothing.

After that show Knight and I had lunch from time to time. One day he called me and said that he knew I liked horse racing, so why didn't I come out to the track that Sunday morning and watch his horse work out and then have breakfast? It sounded great to me. He had his limo pick me up, we watched the horses and then over breakfast he asked me if I'd like to write a column for the *Herald*. Although I've never gone after professional advancement, I've never turned it down when it came my way. I told Knight I would like very much to write for the *Herald*.

Although Knight tried to maintain a hands-off policy with the *Herald*, it was well known that if Mr. Knight wanted something, he got it. A few days after my breakfast with him, I got a call from the paper's editor, John McMullan, inviting me to lunch to talk about a column. He suggested we meet at La Gorce, one of Miami's swankiest country clubs, to which most of the *Herald*'s top executives belonged. Part of its swankiness lay in the fact that it was very careful whom it accepted as members: Jews and blacks at that time were not considered tony enough to grace the membership list of La Gorce, although they could lunch there if escorted by an approved WASP. I told McMullan that I couldn't eat at La Gorce. He said he respected my feelings and took me to a somewhat less swank but nonrestricted club. There wasn't all that much to discuss; Knight wanted me, and that was pretty much that. It was decided that I would continue to do exactly the same sort of column for the *Herald* that I had done for the *Sun*. So in 1967 I started a six-day-a-week column.

As anyone in the newspaper business can tell you, a six-day-a-week column is a lot of writing. But it always went like a breeze for me; I can't recall once having suffered from writer's block. I think the secret was that I was not a professional newspaper person and therefore I felt free to improvise and learn as I went along. I did a variety of things in the column; you have

to when you're writing six days a week. Some days I would do a
nostalgia piece and tell stories from my childhood in Brooklyn.
Another day I would do a thing I called "It's My Two Cents,"
which was modeled on Jimmy Cannon's "Nobody Asked Me,
But . . ." In it I gave one-line opinions on about twenty things.
Everything from where to get the best hashed-browns in town
to what I thought of the President's speech. Another day I
would do something like "Open Phone America" in print: I
would take letters people had written on various topics and re-
spond to them. Still other days I did a sort of gossip column:
who's going to be in town, who's going out with whom. I remember once someone gave me a tip that Jimmy Cagney was
ill, so I just put a little item in the column saying, "I hope
you're feeling better, James Cagney." A week or so later I
got a letter back from Cagney. The salutation was to the
point, to say the least: no "Dear," no "Larry"; it simply
read "King."

The body of the letter was equally direct: "Sick? See attached." Attached was the doctor's report from Cagney's most
recent physical. Eleven pages on James Cagney's body. It left
me convinced that Cagney was one healthy man, and I printed
a retraction in the column. To this day I have never met Cagney, but he is one person I would dearly love to have on my
show.

I also got a chance to take on the *Herald* in the pages of the
Herald. There was a strong belief on the part of the Jewish
community of Miami Beach that a strain of anti-Semitism ran
through the *Herald.* They said that the paper never had anything favorable to say about Miami Beach. I'm not willing to
say there was deliberate anti-Semitism, but things like membership in La Gorce really bothered me, and I said so in the
paper. I also did some speaking at *Herald* functions. I remember on one occasion I laced into it for this anti-Semitic thing.
Although the paper had a lot of Jewish reporters, there were no

local Jewish columnists besides me. I said that I was a real breakthrough for the paper—although it obviously wanted to go slowly, so it had gotten a Jewish columnist with a Gentile name. I remember talking once to John Knight about La Gorce—about how offensive that is. He said he saw my point, but that it's sometimes possible to work effectively from within. I told him minorities have heard that all their lives. Work from within. Just as long as minorities aren't granted access to the "within."

Every major paper does readership surveys to find out what are the best-read sections of the paper. John Knight told me that 87 percent of the people who took the *Herald* read my column, which is an enormously high percentage. There was some resentment of me at the paper, which at first I didn't understand; then I found out that a lot of newspaper people's ambition is to write a column, and there I was, a total neophyte, with a plum assignment. I can understand that. If Bruce Jenner got a talk show just because he was a celebrity, I can see resenting his being in the business without paying dues. But if it turned out that Bruce Jenner was the best talk-show host to come down the pike, I wouldn't have much basis on which to object. My column was not the best thing ever to be put in a newspaper, but in fact I did deliver, so it was easy to let the jealousy roll off my back.

I lost the column in the *Herald* shortly before the Wolfson thing broke. I was told that I was too good to my friends in the column. But there were also rumblings about my situation with Lou, which I think may have had something to do with my firing. Shortly afterward my column was picked up by the city's second paper *The Miami News*. But by then my troubles were so massive that the *News* kept me for only a little while before I went back to the *Sun-Reporter*. After my return to broadcasting in Miami, the *News* picked up my column again, and I wrote for it until I went to Mutual.

*   *   *

One thing I miss now is that I don't do as much public speaking as I did back in Miami, although I get to do some for Mutual. I used to appear as a toastmaster a couple of times a week, and as with the radio show, I just used to go out there and wing it.

The most important thing to know about my approach to public speaking is that I have never given a serious talk in my life. That's the problem with most speakers at conventions and luncheons: you've got a roomful of people who are eating and drinking, they're willing to learn something, but they also want to have a good time, and most speakers come out and start boring people to death with their earnestness.

My speaking career was launched in a roundabout way. A convention of sheriffs was in town, and Dick Gerstein asked me to go along as a surprise speaker. He said that after the main speaker, he would introduce me as Larry King, a reformed criminal. Almost everyone there was from out of town, so the sheriffs wouldn't know right off that I was not legitimate.

Preceding me on the podium was the head of the Miami Crime Commission—an organization set up by the city to keep crime statistics. This guy was the most boring human being who ever lived. He was up there for nearly an hour giving statistics on crime. That was it: he recited numbers and did some civic boosting in an unbearable, droning voice. By the time he finished, the sheriffs' convention was in collective catatonia. Talk about eyes glazing over! I was really worried; I didn't think the Second Coming could rouse this group.

Dick Gerstein gave me a pat on the back for encouragement and walked up to the microphone to introduce me.

"The young man you're about to hear is now a successful

radio talk-show host in Miami. But before he entered this line of work, our next speaker spent most of his life behind bars. He'd like to tell you about some of his experiences and his feelings today about crime."

The response was, to say the least, lukewarm when I went to the front of the room. I hadn't planned anything to say, but I knew I had better get their interest quickly.

"Ladies and gentlemen, I'm in a business in which equal time is mandatory. We just heard from the head of the Miami Crime Commission. Now I'd like to give you the other side of some of those crime statistics.

"The lowest rate of crime of any city in America is in Butte, Montana. I'd like a show of hands of the number of you who want to live in Butte, Montana. . . . Just as I thought, zero. Therefore, we know people like to go where crime is. Our number one crime cities in America are New York, Miami, Los Angeles; and we all love those cities. When you guys heard this convention was in Miami, you ran to get here. Because of the criminals.

"There are a lot of advantages to crime that we never think about. Crime keeps money local. Crime benefits the community. A criminal takes money from someplace, and that money filters through the community; it never goes through the damn Federal Government. The Federal Government has to finance the Miami Crime Commission. . . . Prostitutes. Where do they spend their money? Local beauty parlors. Bookmakers. Where does their money go? Local restaurants, local haberdasheries.

"Criminals keep property values up. There's a community, for example, here in Florida, which has fourteen known Mafia families living there, and its property values have doubled since they moved in.

"And another thing. Nobody in this room wants crime wiped out. If crime is wiped out, you're all out of work. The head of the Crime Commission is working because of crime. The highlight of his speech was the recitation of criminal activity during the last week. Suppose criminals had decided to strike last week? He'd have nothing to say."

The sheriffs and their wives absolutely loved it. The best part of the speech was watching their faces at the beginning as they were trying to figure out whether or not I was for real, and slowly realizing I was poking fun at the whole thing, particularly the atrocious speaker who had preceded me. Then I told them one of Lenny Bruce's great lines: " 'If crime is ever eliminated, and I'm on a breadline, there's one guy in front of me: J. Edgar Hoover.' I agree with Lenny Bruce: it's important for a community to have crime. It creates a lot of jobs, makes tourists happy, keeps property values high. Without crime you have a depressed area. So what I want you gentlemen to get together and do is promote crime; keep crime going; keep this country as attractive for criminals as possible."

At the end of the speech, one sheriff got to his feet and said, "How can we help?"

The speech was such a hit that Gerstein took me with him to a district attorneys' convention in Denver and had me repeat the whole thing.

The key to public speaking is to know your audience. Once I was appointed to a mayor's commission to try to bring baseball spring training to Miami. I had to make a speech on it to the City Council, and the Miami City Council is like no other. It has always had a great public attendance, because lots of retired people would go to the meetings for entertainment and to lobby for senior citizens' programs. They'd come for the day, pass out pastrami sandwiches, and if a subject didn't affect them they'd kibbitz among themselves.

I got up to make my presentation, and not a soul was listening because I was talking about baseball. So I yelled: "Attention! The head of the American League is in favor of Medicare!" I got a standing ovation.

.

ONE OF THE nicest things that happened to me in Miami was developing a friendship with someone who really was famous: Jackie Gleason. Gleason had been on my various shows over the years. I accompanied him on his well-publicized train ride—he hated planes—from New York to Miami when he moved his television show. Gleason was a superb guest. He is not funny in an interview the way Mel Brooks is, who never stops doing shtick or coming up with great lines; Gleason is a comic *actor*; but he is abolutely marvelous when he talks about comedy, analyzes it, which is something few comedians can do. For example, he said there has been only one successful comic in the history of show business who never asked for sympathy; every comic, including Don Rickles, is saying, "Please like me." Gleason said the only comic who didn't say that was Groucho Marx; Groucho never cared whether the audience liked him or not. I once asked Gleason what had gone wrong with Jerry Lewis, who had everything in the world going for him. "Jerry Lewis found taste," Gleason said. Gleason also wanted very much to play Oscar in *The Odd Couple* on Broadway—a part that went to Walter Matthau. I asked him why. "Oscar reacts, and when you're the one who's reacting, you can get a laugh off a laugh. I always thought Art Carney was funnier than me in *The Honeymooners*. I was bizarre, but Carney got to react to my being bizarre, and if you have sensitivity and the ability to react properly, you can't be topped."

As an example of the power of reaction, he told a story about the filming of *The Hustler*, the Paul Newman movie in which Gleason portrayed pool player Minnesota Fats. "We were watching the daily rushes of a scene in which Newman

and I play a climactic game, and he and I are playing and talking through the scene. Also in the scene is George C. Scott,
who has no dialogue at this point in the movie—he's just sitting there watching us play. As we're watching the rushes of
the scene, I turned to Paul and said, 'Who are you watching
now?' and Paul said, 'I'm watching George. Who are you
watching?' and I said *I* was watching George. There we were
having this crucial match at the pool table, both of us doing
dialogue, and we couldn't take our eyes off George C. Scott,
who was sitting there doing nothing, but doing it so beautifully
that he stole the scene."

Gleason was an amazing person to watch when he was in action. I went down to his studio several times to watch the taping of his television show. He had incredible instincts and great
concentration. He's a one-take performer, but he can also turn
it on and off in an instant. I was backstage once watching him
do a television sketch in which he came offstage, where I was
standing, for about a minute. He came over to me and said,
"Listen: after the show let's pick up some pizza at a new place
I just discovered"—then ran back on stage totally in character
again.

IT WAS ALWAYS GREAT to have Jackie as a guest, but he is also
responsible for booking one of the most extraordinary shows
I've ever had.

In 1969 I was sitting in Jackie's living room and he asked me
what would be impossible for me to do in the business. I said it
would be impossible for me to get an interview with Howard
Hughes. I asked Jackie what would be impossible for him.

"Playing a romantic lead," he said. "I could do a 'Marty'-
type character, but never a real romantic part."

"Another impossible for me would be to interview Frank
Sinatra," I added.

At that Jackie perked up. "When do you want him?" he said.

Now, Frank had just opened at the Fontainebleau and was a big, big draw. But he absolutely hated the press and never gave interviews. I told Jackie to cut it out—it would be easier to get Howard Hughes than Sinatra. Jackie simply said, "I asked you, when do you want him?" I assured Jackie that any time that was convenient for Sinatra would be convenient for me.

Within two weeks of that conversation, Jackie called me and said, "Would a week from Monday be okay?" I said somewhat dubiously that it sounded good to me. Jackie replied, "If I tell you you've got it, you've got it."

"Suppose I go back to the station and they start promoting this?" I asked.

"Do it," Gleason said.

I went back to the station and told the general manager and the promotion director the whole story. They tried to call the hotel to confirm it, but they couldn't even get through to a Sinatra flunky. I knew Jilly Rizzo, Sinatra's friend and sort of bodyguard, so I called Jilly and told him about the conversation with Gleason, and Jilly said, "No one tells Frank what to do." Great. In spite of that, because the promise had come from Gleason, who was not a boastful man, we decided to go ahead and promote the show: "Next Monday night at nine o'clock on *The Larry King Show*, Frank Sinatra." If you listened to WIOD, you could not escape this message. I think we secretly hoped that Sinatra, or someone in his entourage, would hear it and believe that Sinatra was going to do the show. The Friday before the supposed show, the station wanted to take a full-page ad in the newspaper. I was getting a little nervous, having heard nothing from anyone connected with Sinatra in the week we had been promoting the show. I called Gleason and told him about the newspaper promotion. "Do it," he said.

Finally, the Monday of the show rolled around. We had promoted the hell out of this thing; people had been calling the station like crazy; the rest of the media were talking about it; still no word from Sinatra. I was at the studio—by that time we had returned the show to the studio from the boat—most of the day, hoping I would get some sort of confirmation, and watching a crowd form in front of the building. It was now about 8:30 P.M. We had a huge sign covering the front of the station: "WELCOME FRANK SINATRA!" We had ropes all over the place to keep the crowd restrained; cops were patrolling the area; photographers were swarming. I realized at that moment that if Sinatra didn't show, it was going to be my neck, not Gleason's.

At a quarter till nine a huge black limo pulled up, and the crowd went wild: they were screaming, waving banners, yelling, "Frankie, Frankie!" The limo door opened, and a man who was definitely not Sinatra got out. I thought we were going to have to get the riot police. The guy came into the studio and introduced himself. He was Sinatra's press guy. "Listen, Sinatra will be here in three minutes. I don't know how you got him, but I came here a little in advance to say a few things," he said.

First, he wanted me to explain the format of the show, which was like the show on Mutual: a live interview, and calls from listeners. But I told him that in deference to Sinatra, there would be no call-in segment that night. Then he asked me how long Sinatra was scheduled for, and I said two hours.

"Bullshit," he said. "You are never going to get that. Maybe you'll get half an hour, forty-five minutes at the longest, but you're not going to get two hours.

"Sinatra pays me fifty thousand dollars a year and I have one job: to keep him out of the press. I get bonuses if he never hears about doing a show like this. If I recommended a show like this, I would be looking for another job. I don't know why he's doing it, but he is, so I want to warn you about one more thing. Do not bring up his son's kidnapping. If you bring up his son's kidnapping, out he walks."

As usual, I had made no special preparations for the show, and I wasn't really thinking about whether or not I would bring up the kidnapping. I was a little surprised the press guy mentioned it; it had happened several years before. But at the time there had been talk, never proved, that his son might have planned the whole thing himself, so I guessed Sinatra was still sensitive about it. I didn't have too much more time to think about it, because at that moment another limo pulled up. Nine guys got out of this limo, and in the middle was Sinatra. The crowd surged around him, and the cops pushed them back, and Sinatra and his crew rushed into the studio. We were introduced. Then Sinatra said, to no one in particular, "It's a little warm in here"—at which point all his flunkies ran for the air conditioning. It was funny to watch: eight grown men desperately looking for a thermostat. Then we all went into the studio. Sinatra took his seat, I took my seat and Sinatra said he thought it would be best if just the two of us and the press guy were in the studio, so the rest of them all ran for the door. We had a minute or two before we went on, and as we were waiting for the news to end, Sinatra said, "Jackie says wonderful things about you.

"I'll tell you why I'm here," he continued. "Eighteen years ago I was working at the Town and Country in New York and we needed a comic to open the bill. Jackie was working at a small club in Jersey—he was not well known at the time—and the guy who was supposed to open for me got sick. I'd heard of Jackie, so I called him and asked him to do the show as a favor. Every night he had to do his show in Jersey, drive to New York, open for us, drive back to Jersey for his second show, then back into the city for our second show.

"I told him then, 'I owe you one.' He called me about a

week ago and said, 'Remember the Town and Country? Here's the one you owe me. Do this show.' "

Then, bang! the announcer said, "And now, Larry King." It was another occasion in which I knew after five minutes I'd got him. We started talking about singing. I asked him what it is that he does that other singers don't do; phrasing, how he learned that. Instead of saying that he tried to mimic the sound of a particular singer, he said that as a kid he used to take home Yehudi Menuhin violin albums and listen to them for hours on end and try to re-create the quality of the violin with his voice—"because when Menuhin played a sad song, he could really make you sad." Then when Sinatra joined the Tommy Dorsey orchestra as a young man, he said he tried to do the same thing with the orchestra: listen to how the instruments created various emotions, and try to get that quality into his singing.

We spent the first hour talking about singing, and it just rolled by. Sinatra was all smiles, couldn't have been more gracious. His p.r. guy looked stunned. We broke for commercial and came back for the second hour, and I brought up his years in Hollywood. Sinatra told a story about Humphrey Bogart, whom he absolutely idolized.

"The greatest sign I've ever seen in my life was on the door of Bogart's house," he said. "The sign was by his doorbell, and it read, 'It better be important.' You read that, then go ring that bell. The only reason I've never put the same thing next to my door is that I've never liked to copy people."

So the second hour was going well when I said to him—I'll never forget the question—"This thing between you and the press. Is it overblown, or have you really been given a raw deal by them?"

"It's probably been overblown," he said, "on my side and their side. But I've been given a raw deal too. Take my son's kidnapping . . ."

I thought the press guy would fall off the chair. I had never mentioned the forbidden subject—Sinatra did. We did ten minutes on the press coverage of his son's kidnapping: how he had felt exploited during this private, difficult time; how he resented the circus atmosphere; and what it's like to read the sort of allegations that were later made about his son.

What occurred there was a good lesson for an interviewer. The microphones had disappeared, and he was feeling safe with me. That way you are going to learn a lot more. If I had begun that interview by saying, 'What about the kidnapping?' he'd have walked out and we would have learned nothing. Now, I never expected him to mention the kidnapping, and out of courtesy, I wasn't going to bring it up; but because we had developed a rapport, I think I could have brought it up after we'd gotten through the first hour. I would have said, "Before I started this show, your p.r. guy said not to ask about the kidnapping. If you don't want to talk about it, I understand. But why did he have to say that to me? Then Sinatra could have said, "Sorry, I don't want to talk about it," or he could have made the points he made about being treated unfairly by the press, but he wouldn't have walked out.

I know there are interviewers, good interviewers, who have a totally opposite approach, but they also get something different from their subjects. Mike Wallace, for example. Sinatra would not go on with Wallace. But Mike works off a different kind of ego. What happens with Mike Wallace is that people go on with him because they feel He has made a fool of everyone else, but he's not going to make a fool of me. And Mike likes that sort of challenge. Mike is also totally prepared—has prepared all his questions. I like to be surprised myself by what develops, what I'm going to ask. I would go on with Mike Wallace thinking I'm the one guy he won't make look like a dope.

But what I did with Sinatra was create trust, so when the

microphones disappeared I still had control. And part of the reason I had his trust, besides Gleason's having recommended me, was that I really cared about his music. All of us care about what we do, and when I show someone I'm really interested in what he does, I've got him.

A FEW YEARS LATER I had another encounter with Sinatra which really brought home the impact of being such a public figure. I was emceeing the opening of one of his movies—in those days there were still elaborate movie premieres in which the star showed up. The crowds were four and five deep lining the approach to the theater, and my job was to introduce the stars as they came up and talk to them for a few minutes before they went inside. The crowd was excited, but certainly in control until Sinatra drove up. Then things went wild. What was funny about it was that these weren't by any means schoolgirls. These were, for the most part, middle-aged Jewish ladies, who had probably been screaming schoolgirls when Sinatra was first popular. In any case, he still had the old magic, because as soon as he stepped up to my microphone, they went berserk and rushed the barricade. Suddenly, the two of us were shoved together bodily, and we were both being dragged into the theater by the crowd. His head was jammed into my neck, but I still had my microphone, so I started giving commentary as if I were covering some sort of disaster: "All that can be seen now is the popcorn . . ."

I have to admit that I understood vicariously the thrill there must be in being able to arouse a mass of people to such a pitch. But the problem with that sort of fame is that you become its captive. I'm sure Sinatra doesn't want the adulation ever to stop. But there must be times when he wishes he could go out for an ice cream, or to the movies, and not have to worry whether he'll get home in one piece.

*   *   *

ANOTHER MEMORABLE show-business guest was comedian
Mel Brooks. In those days Mel had not achieved the international fame he has today. He was known for his writing on the
Sid Caesar show, and for his two-thousand-year-old man, but
he had not made any of the movies that brought him his greatest success. Mel was always "on," always doing wild routines—it was impossible to get a straight answer out of him;
but it really didn't matter because he was so funny. He was
also exactly the same on and off the air. Once, after the show,
he invited me to go out to dinner with him and his wife, the
actress Anne Bancroft. They were staying at the Fontainebleau, and the two of us took a limousine to the hotel to pick
her up. Suddenly, on the way to the hotel, Mel said to me in a
stage whisper, "Get down, get down." He ducked down so his
head was below the level of the front seat, and I did the same.
"Mel," I said, "why are we sitting like this?" And he said,
"Jews and limousines don't mix. If you're a Jew, never trust a
ride in a limousine. Did you see our driver? He looks like his
name is Helmut. If he takes us somewhere where there's a
shower, do not get in that shower."

Finally we got to the hotel. Anne had had a tooth pulled
earlier that day, so she was not feeling too well, but Mel called
her from the lobby and asked her to meet us. At this time Mel
was not a famous face, so no one paid any attention while we
were waiting. When the elevator doors opened and Anne came
out, out of nowhere Mel was yelling and pointing: "My God!
It's Anne Bancroft. Academy Award–winning actress Anne
Bancroft!" Naturally a crowd gathered and started asking for
autographs. She signed them all very graciously, while swear-
ing at him under her breath. Mel then went over to a guy who
was obviously in town on some convention and said to him,
"Did you see who that was?" And the guy said, "Yeah, it's

Anne Bancroft. . . . You know, I heard she married some Hebe."

When I left Miami to go to Mutual, some of the guys at the station put on a roast for me and had some of the celebrities I'd interviewed call during the roast. Mel was one of them. He started off very sincerely: "Larry, this is a great opportunity for you, and we're all delighted and know the show will be a big success. It's just too bad that you still can't come to California because the girl isn't sixteen yet. Now, it's only a pending charge, and I'm sure it's totally unfounded and will not interfere with your show at all. They've still got the hotel room sealed because of the investigation. But Larry, everyone in this community loves you. . . . Eleven years old, Larry—the girl was eleven years old . . . but Larry . . ."

Mel has an absolutely spontaneous sense of humor. He has funny genes. During the 1964 World's Fair in New York, I was doing my radio show from the Florida pavilion, and Mel was my guest one day. I had always thought his two-thousand-year-old-man albums were the greatest comedy albums ever made, so I decided to ask Mel, as the two-thousand-year-old man, if he'd ever been to the World's Fair before. Mel went immediately into the routine, with me playing the Carl Reiner straight-man part.

"What do you think of this World's Fair?" I asked.

"It's okay, but not as good as the first one," he replied.

"When was the first one?"

"First World's Fair was in 0082. We had a hundred-percent attendance; the whole world came: seven hundred and thirty-two people."

"Where was it held?"

"The bottom of a ravine. In those days there was no transportation, so people had to roll in. That was one of the exhibits, watching them roll in."

"Now, wait a minute. What kind of fair could you have in

0082? Have you seen this World's Fair? We have trips to the
moon; we have homes that take care of themselves. What
could you have had at the first World's Fair?"

"Are you kidding? We had the burning bush. You jump on,
and you jump off. We thought it was a ride. You want a hit?
I'll give you a hit. We had the Chariot of Jericho; was that a
hit! You ever see anything like that?"

"What was the biggest thing at the Fair?"

"Oh, the biggest thing, easily, was Moses parting the Red
Sea. He did it five times a day, six on Sunday. A great attraction; great showman."

"Did you know Christopher Columbus?"

"Crazy Chris? With the knickers? What a sweetheart; probably the best dancer in Italy. He did the bolero before George
Raft thought of it. Won all the contests. But a crazy man; he
had crazy, crazy ideas.

"Why did Queen Isabella give him the money to buy
ships?"

"You don't know? Chris took the money from her under
false pretenses. Queen Isabella gave him the money to take an
apartment in Paris. She figured they'd go dancing, fool around
a little."

"Do you remember the day he said the earth was round?"

"Remember? How could I forget? I was sitting in the court-
yard and crazy Chris walked in with the knickers and said,
'The earth is round.' I laughed so hard I spit out my whole
tuna-fish sandwich."

"Did you know Henry Ford?"

"Henry Ford? I gave him the idea."

"Whoops, hold on, wait just a minute. You gave him the
idea . . ."

"No, no, wait a minute. I don't want to take full credit. He
came up with the idea for the engine. I had an idea to take the
tire and screw it onto the horse's leg; that way the horses would

last longer, because they would roll—they wouldn't have to run as hard."

I had Mel do the two-thousand-year-old man on another occasion back in Miami. On this particular show Norman Vincent Peale, the minister and author, was the first guest. Then I had Mel come on and go into the two-thousand-year-old man. Neither of us knew what Peale's reaction would be when I asked Mel if he had known Jesus.

"Know him? What a sweetheart! Skinny little kid. I felt so sorry for him I used to give him water when he came in the shop."

"Was he a good carpenter?" I asked.

"Oh, the best. He made a chest of drawers for me. Three fake drawers and three real drawers—a beautiful job. Charged me sixteen drachmas for it. If I'd only kept the cancelled check! But who knew he'd be a smash?"

Peale was absolutely on the floor. Gleason once said about Mel that to be able to go into that character, to take questions without having any preparation, you have to be a genius. And part of Mel's genius is that he has such a breadth of knowledge that he can play off fact; he really knows the history he's parodying.

Mel has changed quite a lot since the days when I knew him during the sixties as a struggling filmmaker and writer. It's probably a combination of age and success, but he is not the perpetual-motion machine he was then. Of course, he is every bit as brilliant as he ever was, only today he is comfortable enough to say some serious things alternately with the shtick.

I had Mel on the Mutual show in 1981, and before we did the show, Mel, Sharon, Herb Cohen and I all went out to dinner at the Palm, a well-known Washington restaurant. Now, the crowd at the Palm sees important people eating dinner there every night of the week, and the other patrons are much too cool even to bat an eye, but they weren't cool when it came to Mel. People came up to him for autographs and there was a lot of staring at him and whispering about him. Mel was gracious throughout the entire thing, but at one point he said, "I really don't like people looking at me. I'm basically a writer, and a lot of my success is based upon my observations. But it's very hard to observe people when they're observing you."

The Palm is known as a steak house, and everything it serves comes in enormous portions. Mel said he was trying to lose some weight, and he ordered hardly anything. He then proceeded to eat half of Sharon's meal. Believe me, that's very Jewish.

When he was taking calls, Mel exposed a tender side you don't often see. One caller wanted to know how his marriage to actress Anne Bancroft managed to be a success.

"There is no clash of egos in my marriage," he said. "I could never be what she is. She is one of the greatest actresses we've ever had. If we both died today, she'd get top billing in the obituary."

ANOTHER NOTABLE YOUNG PERFORMER also appeared on the Miami show when, like Mel, he had yet to reach the height of his fame. I was told an actor named Dustin Hoffman was doing a tour promoting a movie called *The Graduate*. I had never heard of Hoffman or the film when my producer booked him. Dustin was very pleasant, soft-spoken, almost shy. Nothing in the interview made me think I was in the presence of a major star-to-be. When I saw the movie, I was practically knocked off my seat. He has the same quality on screen that Gleason described George C. Scott as having: you can't take your eyes off him.

When Dustin was back in town to film *Midnight Cowboy*, he had become one of the hottest actors around. I called him and asked if he would do the show. He was very polite about it, but declined, saying he didn't want to do anything that would distract him from creating the part of Ratso Rizzo—the low-life character he played in the film. But Dustin did invite me over to his hotel for dinner. He was staying in one of the swank places along the beach, but when I went into his room to see him, he looked like Ratso Rizzo: unshaven, hair long and dirty. He had one leg tied with a string: Ratso Rizzo walked with a limp, so Dustin wanted to know what it was like to limp. We sat in the room talking for a few minutes, and at one point I went over to adjust the venetian blind because the sun was streaming into my eyes. Before I got to the window, Dustin yelled, "No, no, let me do it." He wanted to know what it was like to try to fix a venetian blind he couldn't reach while limping. So he went over and got on a chair and struggled with that damn blind until he finally got it fixed. When I went to see *Midnight Cowboy*, sure enough, there was a scene in which Ratso went over to fix a venetian blind. It was a kick to have been there "at the creation."

I WAS ALSO at another behind-the-scenes moment of inspiration with guest Ralph Nader. Ralph has been on several times on Mutual, but this was the first time I had him on my show, and in the mid-sixties he had just exploded onto the scene and really had people examining their roles as consumers for the first time. I went to pick up Nader at the airport—we were putting him up at the Fontainebleau, which he strenuously objected to, and I have to admit he looked awfully out of place in the gaudy lobby—and on the way into the city we stopped at a tollbooth. I was driving some sort of extravagant car, as usual, with all the accessories, including air conditioning and power windows, and I had had to lower the window in order to pay the toll. As soon as we passed through, Nader got very excited and ordered me over to the side of the road. I didn't know what was happening—I thought he might be having an attack of some kind—so I got out of traffic and pulled over to the side of the road. We were sitting there on the shoulder and Nader took out his briefcase and stopwatch and said, "Do that again."

"Do what again?" I asked, convinced that this guy was totally bananas.

"Lower and raise the window again," he said.

I dutifully hit the button and brought the window down, then up.

"Do it again," he said, even more excited.

So I did it again. He had me do it one more time; then he said, "God, it goes up in less than two seconds. Why does it go so fast?"

"Gee, Ralph, I don't know."

"Let's do it a couple of more times," he said, and I did; then he said, "Look at that. If a kid had his hand out that window, he couldn't pull in his fingers fast enough if someone else was pushing the button. Why does it do it so quickly?"

"Ralph, I really don't know. What are you going to do about it?"

"I'm going to follow up on it," he said.

Later I got a letter from Ralph which contained the responses he got from the automakers when he wrote and asked them why the windows went up so quickly. He had gone out and tested every power window on the market; then he had written to all the medical examiners across the country and asked how many accidents—mangled hands, that sort of thing—had been reported because of automatic windows. The responses from the car manufacturers were unbelievable. No one had a real reason why the window went up so quickly; I'm sure they felt if you're buying power windows, they had better be powerful. But one manufacturer said there was a sexual aspect to the operation of the window, because if it goes up really quickly, it makes a noise when it hits the top, and men liked that sense of power. Nader wrote to them that if they didn't lower the speed with which those windows close, he was going to go public with it, and with the cases of mangled kids. He never had to; if you notice today, automatic windows go up rather slowly. I have one, and it doesn't make any sound when it hits the top; I can't say it's affected my sexuality any, however.

THE SIXTIES were a wild time for me. Although I was not nationally known, I had achieved more success and gotten more recognition than I had ever dared dream about. I also paid a price for that success by not being able to handle it. In part, my problem was due to the fact that everything just fell into my lap. After the reading I did for Marshall Simmonds to get that first job at WAHR, I never went through an audition again; for that matter, I never looked for a job again. The fact that I never had to sell myself, knock on doors in order to advance my career, did nothing to temper my total irresponsibility.

I certainly didn't lack ambition, but I never had anything resembling a career plan. I don't think I was capable then of plotting a career the way kids do today: working eighteen months at a station in the sticks; sending audition tapes to bigger stations; constantly looking for that next move up, the next break. If I had applied more direction to my career, I could probably have gone much further than I did before I landed at Mutual. I'm very lucky in that respect, though: the ideal job found me; I didn't have to go look for it. Of course, if I had been capable of taking responsibility for my career, then I also would have been capable of taking responsibility for my personal life; I wasn't capable of doing either. Until my mid-40s I never dared to think beyond next week.

Afterword

AS I REVIEW MY LIFE at age 48, I am grateful to be where I am professionally. Considering the magnitude of the mistakes I've made, I have to give thanks for my extraordinarily good luck, and that there were people who were willing to give me another chance.

I am in the phase of life that is referred to as "middle age"—which strikes me as somewhat euphemistic, since I can assure you I'm not going to live to be 96. For the first time in my life, I do have a vision, of sorts, of what I would like to be doing ten years from now. My contract at Mutual has four years to run, but after that I would like to stop working all night. It's too disruptive of one's life outside work, and it is much too wearing physically. Every now and then I recall that my father died while working nights, and while I don't necessarily think it is fatal, I know that it has aged me; there is no way around it: I'm chronically tired.

When I'm 58, I would like to have a newspaper column and be doing a one-hour radio interview show and a television talk show on a regular basis. Radio has been my home and I don't want to leave it, but I would like the excitement of a return to television. Twenty years after I started doing interviews, I'm still as enthusiastic about it as I ever was. Recently, I was in Miami and I appeared as the guest on a radio show. During the break the interviewer and I were talking about the business, and he said to me, "I've heard it all." My response was that I haven't heard it all and I hope I never feel that I have.

Whatever I end up doing, I would like to keep my link to younger people. Surveys we've done on the show indicate that about 20 percent of our listeners are students, and that is very heartening to me. I have never, to my knowledge, heard Bruce Springsteen, yet fans of his are fans of mine.

Obviously, one big reason so many students are listening to me is that they are up pulling all-nighters. But it's more than that. If they are up, they certainly don't have to listen to *The Larry King Show.* I'd like to think young people respect me because, like them, I am not cynical. But that doesn't mean I'm not sure enough of myself to tell a caller he doesn't know what he's talking about.

THE MOST IMPORTANT thing in my life now is my daughter, Chaia. Although we are close, it's painful to have her living in Florida. Absentee fatherhood is the worst; no matter how often you talk or visit, it's terrible not to be there, not to have day-to-day control. This is compounded by the fact that anyone with any inkling of what it is like to be a teen-ager today— what has become accepted behavior, such as drugs and sex— would prefer to see his or her children skip the whole terrible business. For example, Chaia, a high school freshman, has been infatuated recently with a senior—an infatuation he apparently reciprocates. I called her one night and Alene told me that Chaia was having dinner at this fellow's house. Well, I got very upset at hearing that, Alene's assurances that he was a very nice boy notwithstanding. I don't care how nice a boy he is, I was 17 once and I know what 17-year-old boys are like and I don't want my 14-year-old daughter having anything to do with one. I have to admit that a lot of the things I got so sick of hearing my mother say about the agonies of raising children have turned out to be true.

On another occasion I took Chaia with me on a trip to New York. We had a wonderful time seeing Broadway shows, visiting museums and touring my old neighborhood. To give her a taste of the glamour and decadence of New York, I also took her to the disco Xenon one night. It was as wild as it had been billed, and Chaia loved every minute of it. We were sitting at our table taking in the scene when a very good-looking boy of about 19 came over and asked Chaia to dance. Chaia was about 13½ then but looked, when she got dressed up, about 18. She asked me for approval, and I let her go. There I was, sitting in a New York disco watching my 13-year-old on the dance floor next to Mick Jagger—yes, he was there that night—and the thing that killed me was that she fitted right in. Watching her, I started to get really bugged because she knew all the steps. How does a 13-year-old learn how to dance like that? After about twenty minutes of this I got up, went to the dance floor, took her by the arm and escorted her out of Xenon. What the evening really brought home to me was that to me my daughter will always be 8 years old: that's how I still envision her. It is not easy to come to terms with the fact that she is turning into an adult.

I have no specific wishes for Chaia. Right now she talks about being a veterinarian, and I think that would be great. But whatever she decides to do, I hope for two things: that she realizes her potential, and that she doesn't do anything to hurt

herself. I feel confident about both these wishes. She is an in-
tuitive, mature person who has been able to learn from the
weaknesses in the adults around her. To be honest, I do have
one specific wish for Chaia: I would like her to go to college
near me; that would be a great time in which to have her close.

MY YEARS AT Mutual have been wonderful not only for the
professional opportunity they have brought, but for the education I have gotten from my listeners from all over the country.
Though I hear an increasingly dark view of the future, I take
comfort in the intelligence of the American public and their
concern for the issues. When people point out that only half
the eligible voters vote in the presidential election, I have to
believe it's not from apathy, but from a dislike of the choice
offered. I say that because week in and week out I hear from
people on topics ranging from our educational system to the
arts to the future of the Democratic party. And not only are
the callers informed, but many of them are active in behalf of
their concerns. I realize there is a cliché that people get the
leaders they want and deserve, and that's what puzzles me
about the gap I see between the quality of the people I am exposed to and that of our leaders. I have no answers as to why
this is the case, but it concerns me that it's so hard to name
truly great men and women in public life today. When I was
growing up there were giants in the Senate: Taft, Vandenberg,
Humphrey. Name their equivalents today. Quick—name the
Reagan Cabinet. When I was young we knew who the people
were in F.D.R.'s Cabinet; they were important figures. The
same thing goes for industry. School kids used to know the
heads of our major corporations; how many can the average
teen-ager name today?

This gap between the public and its leaders was demon-

strated for me when I had a Ford Motor Company executive
on the show a few years ago. This was just before the automakers put on their big push, in part mandated by government
mileage rules, to build smaller cars. Out of the first fifty callers
forty-five had foreign cars. It became almost comic: "Hi, I own
a Toyota." "Hello, I'm a Volkswagen driver." "Hi, I have a
Honda." But it also did a lot to explain why the American au-
tomobile industry is in such pathetic shape. These people almost all said they would prefer to buy an American car, but
either they weren't willing to sink thousands of dollars into another lemon or they couldn't afford to drive a big car. What
was most pathetic, however, was that this executive was
shocked by what he heard. What in the world did he think was
going on? Didn't he ever bother to look out his own car window and wonder why he found so few Fords on the road?

The concerns of my callers, and particularly their fears, have
affected my thoughts about the future. I get quite a few calls
on new technology, many of them from people involved in the
technology themselves, but tempering the excitement about
technological breakthroughs is a fear of what it will mean to
our privacy. There is a deep-seated distrust of computers,
even—or especially—as they assume a larger role in our day-
to-day lives. People are concerned that their Social Security
number will become a total identification number; that with it
it will be possible to find out practically everything about their
lives. As someone who has lived a more or less public life for a
number of years I understand that concern. Americans are
afraid they may be unwittingly trading control over what people know about them for the convenience that technology
offers.

The greatest fear I hear expressed is that of nuclear weapons.
I hear more and more talk about the inevitability of a nuclear
confrontation. If it doesn't happen between the United States
and the Soviet Union, people are afraid some terrorist group or
demented dictator will use a nuclear bomb.

I find myself being changed by concerns such as these voiced by my listeners. I catch myself talking of inevitability in my own private conversations. I remember one caller's saying that at a certain point each side's having nuclear weapons is a deterrent. But after you cross a threshold in the number of weapons you have and the resources spent on producing and maintaining them, instead of acting as a deterrent, it encourages a tendency to use the weapons. If my caller is right, it's chilling to speculate when we will cross—or whether we have crossed—that threshold.

There is another aspect of the nuclear question which again demonstrates that the public is more sensitive and intelligent than its leaders: that is this whole notion of a nuclear war's being winnable—a notion now discussed at the highest levels of government. The public is frightened by that, and rightly so. What does it mean to talk about a major nuclear confrontation's being winnable? That every speck of life is not destroyed? The most frightening thing about an adoption of this belief by our leaders is that, as my caller pointed out, it creates a set of mind that makes nuclear confrontation all the more likely.

Another thing I have learned about Americans from doing my show is that they really admire honesty and are willing to forgive a lot if people will just own up to their mistakes. If my listeners heard the words "I'm sorry," from politicians more often, politicians would be held in much higher regard.

I've also discovered just how egocentric Washington really is. Matters that obsess the press here and are the subject of endless discussion at dinner parties can be of little concern to people outside Washington. For example, I have not had one call on Nancy Reagan: whether she's a snob, too extravagant, too clothes-conscious. Nancy Reagan gets plenty of licks in Washington; it's significant to me that none of my callers, who talk about every subject under the sun, has ever bothered to mention her.

Although most of what I have learned of America by doing the show has been positive, I am not completely sanguine. Racism is far, far less virulent than it was twenty years ago. The ugliness that surrounded the civil rights movement, which I remember well from my days in Miami, has abated a great deal, but racism has by no means disappeared. I get many callers who are against busing, but if you scratch below the surface, what is being said is "I don't want my kids to go to school with blacks." Once, on the show, I had a man call who was railing against affirmative action, or something similar, but his real message was that he didn't like blacks. I told him a story that had been told to me by a black civil rights activist years before in Miami. This activist had been a soldier in the Army during World War II, stationed on our southeastern coast. It seems that a German submarine was picked up off the coast and the German prisoners of war were put in custody of his unit, which was to escort them to a prison camp. During the trip to the camp, the unit stopped at a restaurant for a meal. The Americans and the Germans all went into the restaurant—with the exception of a black G.I., because the restaurant didn't serve "coloreds." I said to my caller, "You think about that and maybe you'll understand why blacks are angry." The caller paused, and then said two words before hanging up: "Thank you."

Moments such as that—when you can really get to someone, force the person to reevaluate his thinking—are rare, but when it happens it's thrilling.

I am also hearing increasing sentiment against Israel. I don't believe that it is my obligation as a Jew to blindly support every Israeli policy, but perhaps as a Jew I am more sensitive to Israel, so I am disturbed by this turn of events. I often hear that if the P.L.O. were less violent—a notion that is somewhat naive, since its method is terrorism—Americans would willingly support it. I don't know what the answer to that is, but I do know that supporters of Israel—Jew and non-Jew—must be vigilant. And, I think, must do a better job of explaining their point of view.

EVEN THOUGH I am grateful for the opportunities in broadcasting that I have had, I still harbor some fantasies about what I would like to do. My number one, and lifelong, fantasy is to be a major-league announcer for a baseball team. I don't care what team or even how good they are; it would simply be the fulfillment of a dream to be able to spend a season with a ball club. And unlike most Walter Mittyesque dreams, this is something I would actually be good at. I would like to bring my humor and irreverence to team announcing. Most team announcers are much too solemn. Baseball, after all, should provide an escape from one's cares.

There are also some people I dream of interviewing. They are, in no particular order: Laurence Olivier, because I like actors and like discussing their craft, and in my talks with many actors over the years it is Olivier they've mentioned again and again as the master; J. D. Salinger, because *The Catcher in the Rye* is *the* novel of my era, and because he refuses to be interviewed; Muammar Qaddafi, because he's a fanatic, and I like to get to the core of fanaticism; Reagan and Brezhnev, because they're there; the head of Sony and three or four other top Japanese companies, to find out how they make their companies work; and Elizabeth Taylor, because she is a Star—capital S.

If I am going to indulge in fantasies, then I'll give a partial list of historical figures I'd like to interview: Jefferson and Washington, our fathers: Churchill, to hear him talk about the war; Roosevelt, to find out what it was like to change America; Joan of Arc, for the same reason as Qaddafi; Madame Curie, to find out about the process of scientific discovery; Lenin, Freud and Darwin, to find out what it is like to reshape the world; Columbus, to find out where he thought he was going and how he felt when he got here; Lincoln, not just to talk about the Civil War, but to talk about death, which is something he brooded about a lot; and God—I would ask God one question: "Why?" and then permit him to ramble.

Of course, because of my interviews with Mel Brooks, the two-thousand-year-old man, I have had the pleasure of hearing firsthand accounts of many of these people.

I am not by nature an introspective person, but as I evaluate my life thus far and look to the future, I hope I will take better care of my relationships with others and of my talent. I don't know if my demons are gone, but I do know they're channeled. I make more money than I ever had, which might be considered peanuts when you look at the salaries of some television people, but to me is a lot of money. I don't care about yachts or Alfa Romeos, so I don't have to stroke my ego anymore by living far above my means. The living my income provides me now is a nice one indeed. I have the betting under control as well—not that I was ever a compulsive gambler: again, the track was more a place where I could feel like a big man than anything else. But I still love the horses and go occasionally and take $50 to $100, and that's all. I can afford to lose $100. I don't have to lie about it anymore, or put myself in hock.

Of course, there are things that can never be undone. I regret deeply not having been a better son. My mother died in 1976, and she would have loved to see all the good things that have happened to me since. She always thought I was perfect, but I know I caused her a lot of pain—unnecessary pain. I regret having abused my talent for so many years. That is, I expected to be forgiven my many failings because I was a good broadcaster. By doing that, I showed a lack of respect not only for others, but for myself.

As a kid, when I fantasized about the best possible life I could hope to have, the fantasy was that I was a radio star who hung out at the corner. Well, the corner is gone from my life, and the world of my boyhood no longer exists. Today, when I drive to my house in McLean, Virginia, I drive past Ted Kennedy's house, Roger Mudd's house, the houses of Cabinet officers. As a kid I couldn't have fantasized about the life I have today; I had no idea this sort of life existed.

Sometimes, I have to admit, I still can't believe it exists for me, that I'm living the American dream. Part of me feels that I still belong on the corner. But the problem that has bedeviled me so much of my adult life, and has caused me and others so much grief—the feeling that I was two people: one Larry King, the consummate professional; one Larry Zeiger, the little Brooklyn troublemaker—has abated. I now know that I am living well because I've worked hard to get here. And living the way I do does not mean I have to abandon Larry Zeiger—I can use the energy and mischief of Larry Zeiger constructively in my work.

Above all, what has ruled my life is my twenty-five-year love affair with broadcasting. It's a pleasure, a gift, an honor, to go in front of a microphone and communicate. It's brought me notoriety as well as fame, but always I have felt most alive in front of a microphone, which is something I didn't fully appreciate until it was taken away. As my good friend and fellow eternal Brooklyn boy Bill O'Donnell—the voice of the Baltimore Orioles—says, it sure beats working.